Issues in the Digital Age

Online Privacy

Other titles in the series include:

Online Communication and Social Networking
Online Gaming and Entertainment
Online Information and Research
Online Predators
Online Security

Issues in the Digital Age

Online Privacy

Stephen Currie

San Diego, CA

Printed in the United States

For more information, contact:
ReferencePoint Press, Inc.
PO Box 27779
San Diego, CA 92198
www. ReferencePointPress.com

LIBRARY OF CONGRESS CATALOGING-IN-PUBLICATION DATA

Currie, Stephen, 1960–
Online privacy / by Stephen Currie.
p. cm. — (Issues in the digital age)
Includes bibliographical references and index.
ISBN-13: 978-1-60152-194-1 (hardback)
ISBN-10: 1-60152-194-4 (hardback)
1. Data protection—Law and legislation—United States. 2. Electronic records—Access control—United States. 3. Privacy, Right of—United States. 4. Disclosure of information—Law and legislation—United States. 5. Online social networks—Law and legislation—United States. 6. Government information—United States. 7. Electronic commerce—Security measures. I. Title.
KF1263.C65 C87
342.7308'58—dc23

2011023649

Contents

Introduction

The Complexities of Privacy

Late on a March evening in 2011, someone using the screen name "Doldrum" went online and signed onto a file-sharing website—a service that allows users to exchange pictures, games, videos, and music. While most people who use file-sharing websites have perfectly innocent motivations, Doldrum did not. His intention was to collect illegal images from other users. Specifically, he was looking for pornographic photos and videos of children—images that are not only illegal to make but also illegal to own. Before logging off the Internet later that night, Doldrum successfully downloaded several thousand photos and videos showing children engaged in sexual activity.

What Doldrum did not know, however, was that one of the other people on the site that evening was an officer from the Department of Homeland Security. Upon seeing what Doldrum was up to, he immediately set out to establish Doldrum's true identity. Of course, the name Doldrum was only a pseudonym. But the investigator knew that every Internet connection has a unique identifier known as an IP address. Under police authority, the officer was able to obtain the IP address that Doldrum was using, and from that service provider he obtained the name and address of the Internet connection that had been used to download the photos. The connection turned out to belong to a married couple who lived in Buffalo, New York. Since the vast majority of people who use child pornography are men, investigators decided that the husband was almost certainly Doldrum.

At about six o'clock the next morning, police converged outside the couple's home. Breaking down the door, they stormed into the house, pushed the husband down a flight of stairs, and forced him to lie on the floor. Next, they commandeered the man's desktop computer, along with cell phones and other electronic equipment belonging to him and his wife. When the man asked what was going on, the police accused the husband of downloading the images. The man immediately protested that he was innocent. "I didn't do anything like that," he told the police. The law enforcement team, however, did not believe his story. "You're a creep," they told him. "Just admit it."[1]

The Real Criminal

The case seemed closed; Doldrum had been found. A quick search of the man's computer, however, revealed no sign of the image files. That was something of a surprise, but investigators were sure they had the right man, so they continued to dig. Over the next several days they painstakingly searched all of the couple's electronic devices, looking for the thousands of pornographic pictures and videos Doldrum had downloaded. Again, they found nothing. Although their suspect could conceivably have deleted all the pictures in the brief time since they had been downloaded, the man's computer hard drive should still have shown some digital record of the downloading. Yet it did not. Reluctantly, investigators admitted that their suspect was not the man they had been looking for.

At this point the police looked back at earlier records they had gathered from the file-sharing site. They discovered that Doldrum had logged on to the site several times before—but never from the IP address he had used in March. It quickly became clear that Doldrum did not use his own Internet connections to download pornography. Instead, he tapped into the signals sent by other people's wireless routers. Routers are devices that permit computers throughout a home or public building to share a single Internet access point. They can be very useful when a household has multiple Internet-capable devices. Since the signal from a router can often be picked up 300 feet (about 90m) or more away from the source, members of the household can use the Internet from almost anywhere within the home. Using a router enables more than one person to go online at a time, without paying for more than one modem or other connection.

The 300-foot (about 90m) reach of the wireless signal, however, has one very significant drawback. In most cases, it allows the signal to be

Hackers and thieves have devised many methods for invading a computer user's privacy. Whether working online at home or in an Internet café, personal information may be at risk.

accessed from outside the home—and often from off the property altogether. Thus, anyone near the house who has a laptop or other Internet-ready device can, at least in theory, piggyback onto the signal and use it to go online. Unless access to the router is protected by a password, which the one in Buffalo was not, this type of piggybacking can present a problem for the router's owner. Someone using the signal may not only be able to see what sites the homeowner is visiting online but also potentially capture the homeowner's passwords, account numbers, and other personal identity data. And as the Buffalo case showed, the router's owner is assumed to be responsible for any downloads from that Internet connection.

The story has a reasonably happy ending. Though shaken up by the predawn invasion of his home, the husband was not seriously injured. He was exonerated of any wrongdoing, and he soon received apologies from the authorities in charge of the case. Within a week, moreover, the police had a new suspect—a 25-year-old neighbor of the family who also had connections to the other IP addresses Doldrum had used. As of this writing the man is facing trial for possession of child pornography. If convicted, he could face a sentence of as long as 20 years in prison.

Privacy

The hunt for Doldrum points out a number of important lessons. Among the most significant of these involve the nature of privacy in the online world. On the one hand, the Internet has made it easier for people to commit certain kinds of crimes, of which child pornography is one example. By posting images online, consumers of child pornography can post, download, and exchange images of children in sexual poses in ways that would have been impossible before the digital age. As a law enforcement organization puts it, "The Internet has escalated the problem of child pornography by increasing the amount of material available, the efficiency of its distribution, and the ease of its accessibility."[2]

At the same time, the rise in child pornography is also made possible by a widespread belief that the Internet guarantees anonymity. People seeking to obtain illegal images may think that their true identities will never be known because they use invented, frequently changed screen names and temporary e-mail addresses. The truth is, however, that the Internet is not as anonymous as it would appear. As police grow more and more sophisticated where online crime is concerned, they are better able to use IP addresses and other information to capture criminals—even those who have taken careful steps to disguise their identities. "The same technology used to download and send out these illegal images," notes Illinois attorney general Lisa Madigan, "is now being used by my investigators to track and arrest these offenders."[3]

> **"The same technology used to download and send out these illegal images is now being used by my investigators to track and arrest these offenders."[3]**
>
> — Illinois attorney general Lisa Madigan.

The Buffalo case hinged on one important event: the government's ability to get the Internet provider to match the IP address to the couple it belonged to. Technically, providers are supposed to keep this information off-limits from everyone else. To do otherwise could be considered an invasion of customer privacy. Yet, in a case such as this one, few Americans would be distressed by the government's decision to seek this information. Even though the IP data steered the investigators to the wrong computer, it seems unlikely that many people would quibble with the outcome of the case.

By asking for this information, however, the government raised a number of interesting questions about privacy online, particularly about circumstances in which releasing such data might be less justifiable. After all, it is one thing for the government to invade the privacy of a suspected child pornographer. It may be something else altogether when the government wants to find out who is posting negative comments about a political figure. Similarly, Americans might feel differently if their Internet providers gave customer names and addresses to other businesses—or if the information given out also included social security numbers and birthdates. And Americans might feel differently still if the information they themselves gave to their providers was left unsecured on an online database, allowing thieves to copy it for their own gain.

The question of privacy online, in short, is complex. Very often, how to distinguish an acceptable invasion of privacy from one that should be denounced is far from clear. However, learning to distinguish the two is essential for anyone who hopes to create—or even to live in—a world, digital or actual, that is secure, consistent, and just.

Chapter One

Privacy and the Internet

At the beginning of the 2009–2010 school year, the Lower Merion school system in suburban Philadelphia issued each of its high school students a laptop computer. The computers were intended for use both in school and in students' homes; as district officials explained, the laptops would "ensure that all students have 24/7 access to school-based resources."[4] The machines were well equipped for educational use, with word processing software, graphics programs, and built-in modems for easy connection to the Internet. Students and families applauded the district's decision to issue the laptops. It seemed clear that the machines would link students to the world as well as the classroom, make learning more enjoyable, and improve the overall level of education in the district.

But while students and families were informed about most of the new laptops' capabilities, district officials were silent about one piece of software that had been installed on each computer. This program was a security system known as TheftTrack. TheftTrack was designed to keep tabs on the whereabouts of small, portable computers, such as the laptops used in Lower Merion. If a laptop was reported lost or stolen, district staff could use TheftTrack to remotely activate a small web camera on the missing machine. The camera would then take pictures of the person who was using it and send the images to district servers. By seeing who was in front of the missing computer, district staff hoped to be able to locate and retrieve the machine. The program also took screenshots—still images of what is on a computer screen at any given moment—and sent these captured pictures back to the district as well.

In October 2009 a 15-year-old district student named Blake Robbins set up his laptop on a desk in his room and kept it there for a number of days. A few weeks later, Robbins was surprised to be summoned to see school assistant principal Lindy Matsko. Matsko told Robbins that he had been photographed engaging in "improper behavior in his home."[5] She showed Robbins a photo that pictured him at his desk at home. In the photo, she pointed out, Robbins appeared to be swallowing a small handful of pills, which Matsko and other administrators believed were illegal drugs. When Robbins asked how the district had obtained the photo, Matsko described the TheftTrack system and told Robbins that the web camera had been activated while the computer was in his room. She concluded the meeting by imposing disciplinary action on Robbins.

Robbins was irate. So were his parents when he told them what had happened. The family asserted that the "pills" Robbins was swallowing in the photo were actually Mike and Ike candies. In February 2010 the family filed a lawsuit against the district. The Robbinses charged that district officials had invaded the family's privacy by activating the web camera on a laptop that was neither lost nor stolen—and by not informing the family in advance that the laptops had this feature. To the Robbinses, the notion that district personnel had snapped pictures of their son while in his bedroom was completely unacceptable. "Many of the pictures captured and intercepted may consist of images of minors and their parents or friends in compromising or embarrassing positions,"[6] the lawsuit pointed out.

60,000 Photos

It soon became clear that the Robbinses had a very strong case. An investigation revealed that district personnel had used the web camera in Robbins's laptop to snap photo after photo of the student in his room. Though some of these photos had been deleted by the time investigators checked the computers, several hundred still remained on the district's server. In many of these photos Robbins was asleep. In others, he was wearing only a bath towel. In addition, the screenshots captured by TheftTrack—and therefore visible to district employees—included instant messages, online chats, and other communications with friends that Robbins and his family argued were private and none of the district's business.

Before long, Robbins learned he was far from the only victim of this surveillance. The investigation revealed that district employees had stockpiled at least 60,000 photos of students. Most of the photos showed students at home. All were taken through web cameras without the knowledge or permission of the students or their families. This new revelation provoked growing outrage among students and their parents. "I have my laptop open in my room all the time," Lower Merion High student Savanna Williams pointed out, "even when I'm changing." The district quickly announced that the webcams would be permanently turned off in all school laptops, but Williams was far from mollified. "I've lost a lot of trust in my school district," she said. "I'd like to be reassured that I can get changed in my own bedroom with my laptop open without having to be worried that someone's watching me."[7]

> **"I'd like to be reassured that I can get changed in my own bedroom with my laptop open without having to be worried that someone's watching me."[7]**
>
> — Savanna Williams, Lower Merion High School student.

News of the case was quickly picked up by the media, both in Philadelphia and beyond. Nearly all observers agreed that school officials had showed appallingly poor judgment. Eventually, district leaders came to the same conclusion. In reality, they had little choice once investigators revealed that at least 18 district administrators, technology specialists, and other employees knew about the spying. Some of these staffers, it turned out, were even e-mailing each other to joke about the pictures the cameras were taking. "This is awesome," wrote one woman who worked in the district's technology office. "It's like a little [high school] soap opera." The response from a coworker was "I know, I love it!"[8]

After several months of legal wrangling, the district accepted liability. In the fall of 2010 district officials admitted that Robbins's privacy rights had been violated and settled the lawsuit out of court. The district agreed to change a number of its practices surrounding the laptop program, and it rescinded the punishment it had imposed on Robbins. In addition, it paid the Robbinses an amount believed to be in the hundreds of thousands of dollars. The school district also disciplined several employees for their involvement in the surveillance, though none lost their jobs. Nonetheless, the steps taken by the district were not nearly enough to erase the stain of the scandal. Despite its strong academic programs and its highly rated teachers, Lower Merion is known today in part as the school district where staffers thought it might be fun to spy on students.

Ethics and the Law

The invasion of Blake Robbins's privacy—and the privacy of dozens of other Lower Merion students—was a serious business. Indeed, the Federal Bureau of Investigation looked into the case to see if the people who had carried out the spying might be guilty of criminal charges. However, the bureau eventually determined that the staffers' actions were not illegal. It was against federal law to listen to people's spoken conversations without their authorization, but it was not against the law to view their pictures and written communications. Since the photos and the online conversations had no audio component, the surveillance of the Lower Merion students did not qualify as illegal. In response to this news several legislators called for changes in the law. "I think if you see someone's image and picture that it ought to have the same privacy protections"[9] as oral communications, said Arlen Specter, at the time a US senator from Pennsylvania.

Even though the surveillance was not technically illegal, nearly all observers agreed that it was certainly against ethical standards. Most Americans believe that much of what people choose to do is no one's business but their own. What a person eats, what type of music a person prefers, how parents choose to raise their children—unless the choices a person makes violate accepted ranges of behavior, Americans typically think that people should be allowed to do what they like.

Indeed, the concept of privacy has been central to American thought for generations. Attorney Louis Brandeis, who was appointed to the Supreme Court in 1916, argued that the right to privacy—or, as he put it, "the right to be left alone"[10]—was fundamental to a free society. And while the Constitution does not explicitly guarantee a right to privacy, many interpret the Fourth Amendment as giving privacy a constitutional, and therefore legal, basis. The beginning of this amendment reads, "The right of the people to be secure in their persons, houses, papers, and effects, against unreasonable searches and seizures, shall not be violated."[11]

Privacy is an important American value. The US Constitution (pictured) does not explicitly guarantee a right to privacy, but the phrase "right of the people to be secure in their persons," which appears in the Fourth Amendment, is often cited as indicating that privacy is a constitutional right.

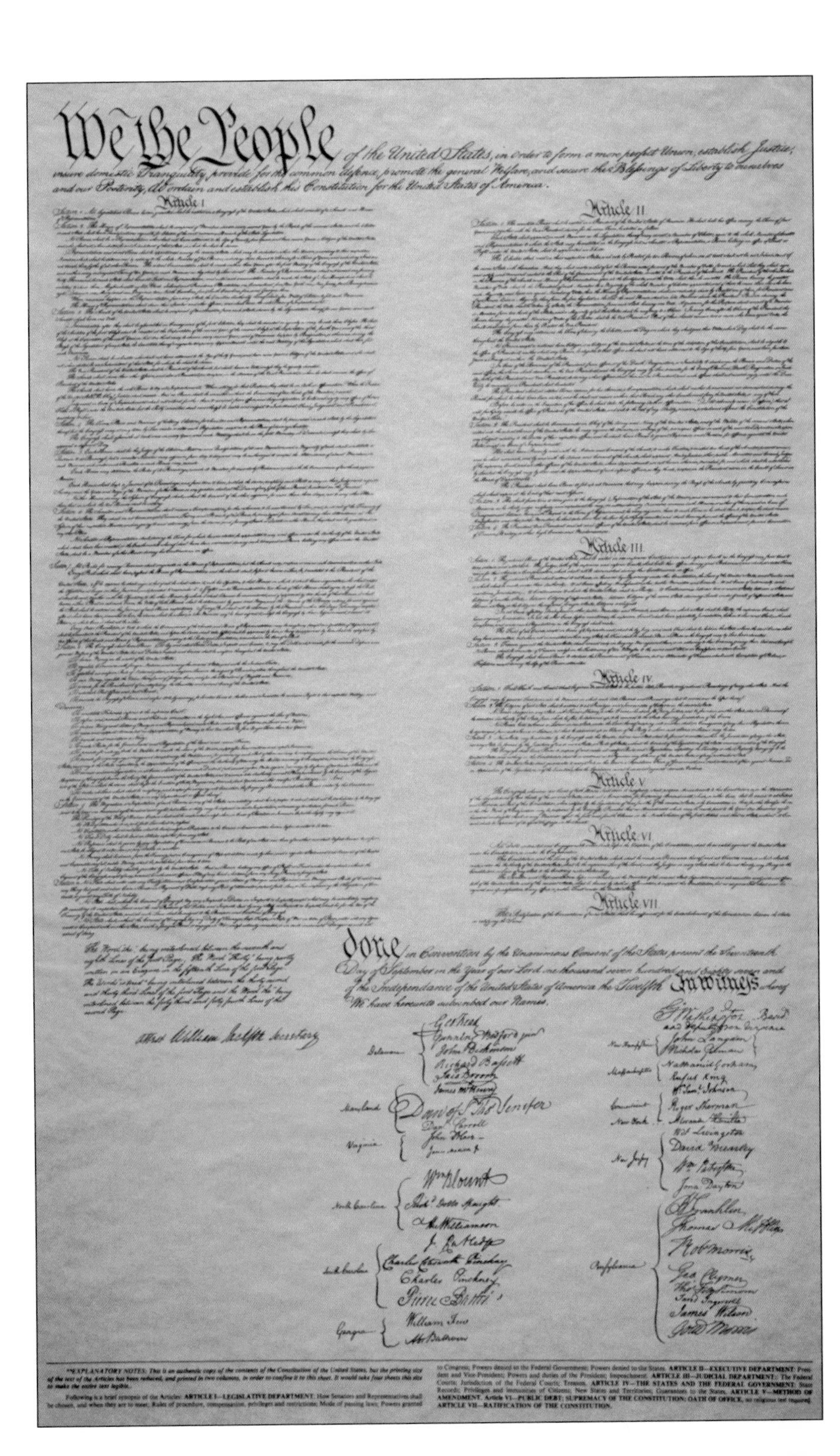

We the People of the United States, in Order to form a more perfect Union, establish Justice, insure domestic Tranquility, provide for the common defence, promote the general Welfare, and secure the Blessings of Liberty to ourselves and our Posterity, do ordain and establish this Constitution for the United States of America.

Article I

Article II

Article III

Article IV

Article V

Article VI

Article VII

done in Convention by the Unanimous Consent of the States present the Seventeenth Day of September in the Year of our Lord one thousand seven hundred and Eighty seven and of the Independance of the United States of America the Twelfth In witness whereof We have hereunto subscribed our Names,

Attest William Jackson Secretary

**EXPLANATORY NOTES: *This is an authentic copy of the contents of the Constitution of the United States, but the printing size of the text of the Articles has been reduced, and printed in two columns, in order to confine it to this sheet. It would take four sheets this size to make the entire text legible.*

Following is a brief synopsis of the Articles: **ARTICLE I—LEGISLATIVE DEPARTMENT**: How Senators and Representatives shall be chosen, and when they are to meet; Rules of procedure, compensation, privileges and restrictions; Mode of passing laws; Powers granted to Congress; Powers denied to the Federal Government; Powers denied to the States. **ARTICLE II—EXECUTIVE DEPARTMENT**: President and Vice-President; Powers and duties of the President; Impeachment. **ARTICLE III—JUDICIAL DEPARTMENT**: The Federal Courts; Jurisdiction of the Federal Courts; Treason. **ARTICLE IV—THE STATES AND THE FEDERAL GOVERNMENT**: State Records; Privileges and Immunities of Citizens; New States and Territories; Guarantees to the States. **ARTICLE V—METHOD OF AMENDMENT**. **Article VI—PUBLIC DEBT; SUPREMACY OF THE CONSTITUTION; OATH OF OFFICE**, no religious test required. **ARTICLE VII—RATIFICATION OF THE CONSTITUTION.**

Moreover, most surveys taken during the 2000s show that privacy rights are supported by a majority of Americans. In one recent poll, for example, 85 percent of respondents said that protecting their privacy when dealing with stores and other companies was important to them. Another survey showed that over half of Americans believed that the federal government should not suspend privacy laws in order to help fight terrorism. As one study of recent polling data puts it, "Public opinion polls consistently find strong support among Americans for privacy rights in law to protect their personal information from government and commercial entities."[12]

The Spread of Information in the Digital Age

The assault on student privacy that took place in Lower Merion can be dismissed as the result of adults behaving both foolishly and badly. Certainly, few observers were willing to defend the actions of district personnel. The district's decision not to inform families about the presence of the web cameras was at best misguided. Matsko's attempt to penalize Robbins for something he may have done while off campus was ill-advised. And of course, the behavior of the employees who activated the web cameras to spy on students cannot be justified. There was plenty of blame to go around. "This is like a black hole of stupid,"[13] one commentator wrote, astonished and appalled by the actions of those in the district who were involved in the case.

At the same time, it is unwise to view the Lower Merion case as simply a terrible mistake, a series of bad decisions that likely will not happen again. The truth is that the case was a uniquely twenty-first-century offense, an invasion of student privacy that was made possible by the digital age. To spy on the students, district personnel made use of a host of technological devices and innovations, many of which did not exist until quite recently. These include web cameras, laptop computers, remote controls, virtual storage space, and of course the Internet itself. In an earlier era, snapping these pictures would have required entering each student's house, installing a camera in a place where it would not be noticed, returning to the house to collect the film, and finally developing

Challenging the Right to Privacy

Some Americans argue that concerns about privacy are overblown. A few commentators believe that by leaving a specific right to privacy out of the Constitution, the founders of the United States were rejecting the notion that such a right should exist. Several politicians charge that the so-called right to privacy has no basis in the Constitution but is instead a creation of judges who misunderstand the Bill of Rights. Rick Santorum, former US senator from Pennsylvania, once referred to "this right of privacy that doesn't exist in my opinion in the United States Constitution," and went on to call it a "right that was created" by judges eager to provide a constitutional basis for new laws that Santorum believes should never have been passed.

Others worry that the emphasis on protecting privacy needlessly handicaps police forces in their fight against crime, particularly terrorism. And to a few observers, arguing for the right to privacy is mainly an excuse for bad behavior. "If you have something that you don't want anyone to know," says Eric Schmidt, the executive chairman of Google, "maybe you shouldn't be doing it in the first place."

Quoted in *USA Today*, "Excerpt from Santorum Interview," April 23, 2003. www.usatoday.com.

Quoted in Cade Metz, "Google Chief: Only Miscreants Worry About Net Privacy," Register, December 7, 2009. www.theregister.co.uk.

and processing the film. This type of surveillance could have been done, but it would have been just about impossible to carry out without being noticed.

The Lower Merion case is only one example among many that show how the Internet has made it more difficult for people to maintain their privacy. Though many of these instances involve web cameras and surveillance, more involve the collection of personal information belonging to individuals. The nature, amount, and variety of this data is unlimited: social security numbers and dates of birth; credit scores and lists of items most often purchased in the supermarket; academic and criminal records; medical and financial histories. Online databases make it easy for corporations and governments alike to store enormous amounts of information about individual people—and make it just as easy to sort and retrieve this information. Today, an entire profile of an individual consumer or taxpayer can be sent around the globe in a matter of seconds.

In the Internet age, moreover, much of this data is easy to amass. Often, people supply it themselves. In the modern world, providing personal information is necessary for carrying out certain online activities. Applying for a credit card, buying a book or a movie online, getting a paycheck or an income tax refund deposited directly to a savings account—all require people to share information such as their home address, age, and bank account number. In other cases, notably on social networking sites such as Facebook and Myspace, people post some of this information of their own accord. User profiles on these sites frequently display hometown, marital status, high school or college, and sometimes much more. In many cases the information can be seen by any interested member of the site.

"You and every other person living today are facing an army of government snoops, corporate data miners, identity thieves, and private investigators, all intent on collecting as much information as they can about you."[14]

— Security expert Duncan Long.

A great number of other people and organizations are interested in this personal information. Corporations use personal data to tailor advertisements to their customers, as well as to determine what merchandise or services to sell in the future. Governments use it to track possible criminals and to compile more detailed demographics of states, localities, and school districts. Hackers, people who access computer systems without authorization, break into computer networks partly in order to steal personal data. As security expert Duncan Long writes, "You and every other person living today are facing an army of government snoops, corporate data miners, identity thieves, and private investigators, all intent on collecting as much information as they can about you."[14]

Online Activities by Age

Percent of Internet users in each generation who engage in this online activity

0–9% | 10–19% | 20–29% | 30–39% | 40–49%
50–59% | 60–69% | 70–79% | 80–89% | 90–100%

Ages 18–33	Ages 34–45	Ages 46–55	Ages 56–64	Ages 65–73	Ages 74+
E-mail	E-mail	E-mail	E-mail	E-mail	E-mail
Search	Search	Search	Search	Search	Search
Health info	Health info	Health info	Health info	Health info	Health info
Social network sites	Get news	Get news	Get news	Get news	Buy a product
Watch video	Gov't website	Gov't website	Gov't website	Travel reservations	Get news
Get news	Travel reservations	Travel reservations	Buy a product	Buy a product	Travel reservations
Buy a product	Watch video	Buy a product	Travel reservations	Gov't website	Gov't website
IM	Buy a product	Watch video	Bank online	Watch video	Bank online
Listen to music	Social network sites	Bank online	Watch video	Financial info	Financial info
Travel reservations	Bank online	Social network sites	Social network sites	Bank online	Religious info
Online classifieds	Online classifieds	Online classifieds	Online classifieds	Rate things	Watch video
Bank online	Listen to music	Listen to music	Financial info	Social network sites	Play games
Gov't website	IM	Financial info	Rate things	Online classifieds	Online classifieds
Play games	Play games	IM	Listen to music	IM	Social network sites
Read blogs	Financial info	Religious info	Religious info	Religious info	Rate things
Financial info	Religious info	Rate things	IM	Play games	Read blogs
Rate things	Read blogs	Read blogs	Play games	LIsten to music	Donate to charity
Religious info	Rate things	Play games	Read blogs	Read blogs	Listen to music
Online auction	Online auction	Online auction	Online auction	Donate to charity	Podcasts
Podcasts	Donate to charity	Donate to charity	Donate to charity	Online auction	Online auction
Donate to charity	Podcasts	Podcasts	Podcasts	Podcasts	Blog
Blog	Blog	Blog	Blog	Blog	IM
Virtual worlds	Virtual worlds	Virtual worlds	Virtual worlds	Virtual worlds	Virtual worlds

Source: Pew Internet & American Life Project, "Generations 2010: What Different Generations Do Online," December 16, 2010. www.pewinternet.org.

Privacy and Social Norms

While Americans say they value privacy, their online actions sometimes tell a different story. People on social networking sites are often quite cavalier with their personal information; they frequently post private details they might be better off keeping to themselves. One recent study determined that about one-third of Facebook users post their birthdates on their pages, while 21 percent of Facebook users with children post the children's photos and names. Similarly, while Americans may decry the amount of private information corporations have gathered about them, computer scientist Harry Lewis points out that most Americans are only too happy to provide this data in exchange for lower prices on merchandise, easier access to credit, or the possibility of winning a prize. "We'll give away data on our purchasing habits for a 10-cent discount on a bag of potato chips,"[15] he says.

> **"We'll give away data on our purchasing habits for a 10-cent discount on a bag of potato chips."[15]**
>
> — Computer scientist Harry Lewis.

Safeguarding information that everyone agrees needs to be kept private is another problem. More and more people, for example, are using cell phones to access the Internet. Many of these people keep sensitive information on their phones, information that may include bank records, medical histories, and so on. If one of these phones is lost or stolen, the private data stored on the device can be accessed by someone else. Experts agree that an Internet-compatible cell should have a password or a PIN to keep unauthorized people from accessing this data. However, a 2011 *Consumer Reports* survey found that of every 10 people who use their phones to go online, only two have actually protected their information with a password. "Millions store data on mobile phones," the magazine concluded, "but few take precautions."[16]

Indeed, some experts wonder whether the Internet is changing our understanding of privacy. This perspective is especially common among people who run companies that deal in computer technology and information. "People have really gotten comfortable not only sharing more information," says Facebook founder Mark Zuckerberg, "but [sharing it] more openly and with more people. That social norm is just something that has evolved over time."[17] As early as 1999, moreover, the chief execu-

Technology and the Threat to Privacy

Every advance in technology, it seems, causes a corresponding threat to privacy. As long ago as the 1890s, the growing popularity of small, portable cameras led to charges that they were leading to wholesale invasion of privacy. Amateur photographers, many believed, were destroying the privacy of passersby by shooting pictures on street corners and printing them without express permission from the subjects. In 1968 a Senate report referred to "tremendous scientific and technological developments that have taken place in the last century" which have permitted "the widespread use and abuse of electronic surveillance techniques."

But although these concerns go back many decades, the issue of what one person can do with a picture of someone else looms increasingly large in the world of the twenty-first century. Thanks to the proliferation of digital cameras, cell phones, and wireless networks, a humiliating photo of a friend who is drunk, using drugs, or in a sexual pose can be on the Internet in a matter of minutes, accessible to people across the entire globe. The impact of photos like these has become much greater since the rise of the Internet.

Quoted in Duncan Long, *Protect Your Privacy.* Guilford, CT: Lyons, 2007, p. xii.

tive officer of technology company Sun Microsystems was expressing similar opinions, if less diplomatically. "You already have zero privacy," Scott McNealy snapped at a group of reporters who were asking him about how his company was protecting the privacy of its customers. "Get over it."[18]

Expectations of Privacy

Executives of companies like Sun and Facebook are not the only ones who believe that the definition of privacy is changing, however. Computer scientist Kieron O'Hara, for example, is worried about the impact of more and more social networkers sharing details about their lives with anyone who happens along. "If you look at privacy in law," he writes, "one important concept is a reasonable expectation of privacy. As more private lives are exported online, reasonable expectations are diminishing."[19] If enough individuals choose to post their birth dates on Facebook, for example, courts may eventually rule that birth dates are no longer private information. And author Emily Nussbaum goes further. In her opinion, traditional ideas of privacy are no longer valid. "Younger people," she writes, "are the only ones for whom it seems to have sunk in that the idea of a truly private life is already an illusion. . . . Your employer owns your e-mails. The NSA [National Security Administration] owns your phone calls. Your life is being lived in public whether you choose to acknowledge it or not."[20]

Regardless of the opinions of people such as Nussbaum and McNealy, most Internet users do have an expectation of privacy when carrying out their online activities. They expect that the information they provide will be used only in ways that they authorize. When they send an e-mail, for example, Americans typically assume that the message will be seen only by the intended recipient. "We're used to thinking of mail as private," notes Long, "and we also write and receive e-mail in a relatively private way."[21] Similarly, customers of an online business expect that the credit card numbers they provide when making purchases will be guarded closely to ensure that this private data is not accessible to anyone else. And while most Americans recognize that governments have good reason to gather and store certain bits of information about citizens, few would feel comfortable knowing that this information was available to anyone who wanted it.

> **"You already have zero privacy. Get over it."[18]**
>
> — Sun Microsystems CEO Scott McNealy.

Like most other parts of life, the online world contains both advantages and pitfalls. No one doubts that the Internet has brought Americans a host of benefits: easy worldwide communication, almost immediate access to information, and much more. At the same time, as the Lower Merion case suggests, the Internet has made it far easier for governments, corporations, and individual people to compromise the privacy of their citizens, customers, and friends. In an era when everything from high

Facebook founder Mark Zuckerberg believes people have become more comfortable with the idea of sharing information in the digital age. This view is reflected in the company's mission statement, which appears behind Zuckerberg at a recent conference.

school grades to medical records can be stored online, the potential for unauthorized use of this information is enormous—and the consequences of such use can be extremely high. Besides using web cameras to spy on people, potential abuses of privacy in the online era include theft of people's personal information, the posting of embarrassing pictures of other people to websites, the sale of data by government agencies to private corporations, and much more. Privacy has always been a concern for Americans. But the Internet age has made the safeguarding of privacy a bigger issue than ever before.

Chapter Two

Social Networking

Although Philadelphia, Pennsylvania, is often called "the City of Brotherly Love," its sports fans have the reputation of being anything but loving. Philadelphia fans are known not only for booing opposing teams, but for being extremely critical of their own players, coaches, and team ownership as well. Philadelphians seem to take particular delight in disparaging their baseball team, the Phillies, and their football team, the Eagles, but no local sports franchise escapes the wrath of Philadelphia fans. In 2009, noting this long history of disapproval, President Barack Obama jokingly awarded Philadelphians the dubious title of the "toughest fans in sports,"[22] and many commentators would agree.

Therefore, few were shocked when in early 2009 an Eagles fan posted an angry rant about his team on the social networking site Facebook. The fan was deeply critical of the way the Eagles were treating one of their best players, star safety Brian Dawkins. Though Dawkins had spent the previous 13 years with Philadelphia and had made seven Pro Bowl teams, the Eagles decided not to bring him back after the 2008 season. Instead, Dawkins signed a contract to play for the Denver Broncos. After the signing was announced, the fan wrote on his Facebook page that he was "devastated about Dawkins signing with Denver." The post then went on to criticize Eagles management, calling team officials "retarded."[23]

The post was written in the heat of the moment. Later that day the fan deleted the comment. However, someone associated with the Eagles saw his post before it was removed. The fan, who had spent the previous six seasons as a part-time staffer for the Eagles, soon got a phone call from the team's front office informing him that he was being fired. He tried to make amends for the posting. "I shouldn't have put it up there," he told a newspaper reporter. "I apologized for it. I apologized 20 million times."[24] However, his apologies failed to move team officials, and he was not reinstated. An overly critical Internet posting had cost him his job.

Social Networks

The site where the Eagles criticism was posted, Facebook, is the most popular of a growing number of social networking sites on the Internet. These sites enable people to connect with each other online. Membership

When the Philadelphia Eagles decided not to bring back star safety Brian Dawkins (center), a loyal fan angrily denounced that decision on Facebook. The fan, who also happened to be a part-time Eagles employee, lost his job after team officials became aware of the post.

is usually free and is most often open to adults or to adults and teenagers. In many cases a prospective member needs only a valid e-mail address to join. After signing up, the new member typically establishes a profile including contact information, basic personal data (such as age, gender, and location), and interests. Members are then able to post opinions, photos, videos, and more. In general, this information is searchable by other members; sometimes it is accessible to nonmembers as well. In addition to Facebook, popular networking sites include Myspace, YouTube, and Twitter.

By any standard, social networking sites have been wildly successful. Friendster, one of the earliest social networking sites to attract widespread attention, boasted 3 million members just a few months after its founding in 2002. Industry experts estimate that Myspace is accessed by more than 40 million different Americans each month. A site called LinkedIn.com, which emphasizes helping people obtain business and professional contacts, boasts members in 200 different countries. The largest of them all is Facebook, which in July 2010 announced that it had reached 500 million members worldwide. Social networking has clearly become an important force in the modern world.

Advantages and Drawbacks

The benefits of social networking are easy to see. For one, sites like Facebook have allowed people to stay in close touch with distant friends and family members. Sharing a photo with people who live miles away, for example, once required making prints of the picture and mailing out copies—a cumbersome, slow, and costly process. Today, in contrast, a photo can be uploaded to a site such as Myspace or Flickr and viewed almost immediately by people across the globe. Social networking has also helped people to connect with old friends and acquaintances, meet new people, and find romantic partners.

However, the effects of social networking have not all been positive. Some of the most serious disadvantages of social networking involve privacy. While most social networking sites allow users to restrict access to at least some of their information, for example, this is rarely the default setting. As a result, a user who wishes to keep information from being accessible to every member of the network must take steps to limit the number of people who can view his or her pages. But the process of putting privacy settings into effect is rarely easy. "Facebook's privacy options are inconsistent to say the least,"[25] complains writer Steve Kovach. Keeping even a semblance of privacy on the site, he points out, requires calling up multiple menus and carrying out a long sequence of steps, few of them intuitive. As a result, many people never bother with privacy settings.

Neither does using privacy settings guarantee that readers will respond positively to what they see. In 2010, for example, Ashley Johnson, a server at a North Carolina restaurant, posted an angry comment about a customer on her Facebook page. Unlike the Eagles fan, whose Facebook posts were visible to anyone who had joined the site, Johnson thought she had taken the time to protect her privacy: She had made her posts accessible only to her Facebook "friends." (Note that a "friend" need not be an acquaintance in real life; in social networking terms, a friend is anyone who asks through the networking site to be added to a member's circle of online contacts and is accepted by the member.) Unfortunately for Johnson, however, not all of these friends were sympathetic to her complaints. One evidently sent the link to Johnson's bosses at the restaurant, who saw her rant and fired her for speaking critically of customers in a public forum. As a labor lawyer put it in the wake of the incident, "The lesson to learn is you don't know who you'll offend—even if they are your friend."[26]

> **"Facebook's privacy options are inconsistent to say the least."[25]**
>
> — Writer Steve Kovach.

Finally, removing a potentially offensive comment, photo, or video from a social networking site is no guarantee that it has not been seen. With the right technology, in fact, anybody is able to preserve a social networking post long past the time when the author has taken it down. "With the ability to take a screen shot of any web page," writes reporter Marie Mariem, "an employer or anyone else with a little computer knowledge can create an immortal record of your status."[27] The moral is clear. In a wired world, it is unwise to assume that any online activity cannot leave traces behind.

Jobs, Insurance, and Divorce

Despite frequent warnings about the lack of privacy on social networking sites, stories such as those of the Eagles fan and the waitress are not

Cyberbullying, Adults, and the Law

Cyberbullying is not limited to young people. In 2006 a Minnesota woman went to a medical clinic seeking treatment for a sexually transmitted disease. Within days, someone posted the reason for her visit on a Myspace page set up specifically to harass the woman. The page included the woman's picture and other details about her life. Whoever posted the page—most likely a worker at the clinic—took it down in a matter of days. Still, the victim was understandably outraged.

The victim tried to use the legal system to punish the worker she believed was responsible for the breach of privacy. She eventually got a court to rule that she was entitled to monetary damages from whoever posted the information. But even being in the right does not ensure that those who invade a person's privacy will actually be punished. In the Minnesota case, the victim never received any payments despite legal recognition that her case had merit. The court was not convinced that the clinic worker the woman suspected had actually set up the page. Since the judges could not determine who was at fault, they did not award monetary damages.

uncommon. Many workers have lost their jobs because of posts on sites such as YouTube and Myspace. In one well-publicized case from 2009, Georgia teacher Ashley Payne posted a picture of herself holding a glass of wine in one hand and a mug of beer in the other. Another posting on the page mentioned a trivia contest that Payne had recently entered; the name of the contest, which Payne quoted, included an obscenity. After someone e-mailed school officials a link to the page, Payne was fired. District officials charged that her page "promoted alcohol use" and "contained profanity,"[28] and in their opinion, both were unacceptable. Payne pointed out that access to her page was restricted, and she argued that she had not listed any of her students or class parents as friends. Nonetheless, her firing stood.

Postings on sites such as Facebook can also prevent people from being offered employment altogether. More and more employers look at the social networking pages of prospective candidates before offering them positions. Applicants who post pictures of themselves using drugs or wearing skimpy clothing may eliminate themselves from consideration, regardless of the strength of their qualifications otherwise. According to one study, about one-third of companies that check applicants' social networking sites have rejected candidates based on something they posted. A cartoon from 2007 sums up the situation nicely: It shows well-dressed professionals begging on a street corner, holding up signs with messages like "Unemployable due to stupid personal stuff I put on my Facebook page."[29]

> **"Some teens are taking great joy in capturing embarrassing images of others."[33]**
>
> — Cyberbullying expert Nancy E. Willard.

Besides causing employment problems, social networking posts have also led to other undesirable outcomes. In 2009, for example, Nathalie Blanchard of Quebec, Canada, went on sick leave from her job due to a diagnosed case of severe depression. Blanchard's diagnosis made her eligible for disability payments from her insurance company while she was out of work. After going on leave, however, Blanchard posted several photos of herself on her Facebook page, including a picture of herself at a birthday party and some photos taken on a beach. In each of these photos she was smiling. Staffers at her insurance company saw the photos, noted that Blanchard seemed to be enjoying herself, and concluded that Blanchard could not possibly be depressed. Accordingly, they stopped paying her benefits. Blanchard then sued her insurer. The case has yet to be resolved, but it highlights the difficulty of determining what is private and what is public on social media sites.

The lack of privacy on social networking sites has also caused major rifts in families. Evidence from sites such as Facebook has been used in thousands of divorce cases. Adulterous spouses have been known to post pictures of themselves with their lovers, for example, in the mistaken belief that they can control who sees this information. Nor do all these cases involve affairs. In 2010 a Maine woman decided to divorce her husband, a recovering alcoholic, because she believed he was drinking again. Though her husband denied it, her suspicions were confirmed by a photo on Facebook—posted by the husband. "Facebook is a great source of evidence," said the woman's attorney. "It's absolutely solid evidence because he's the author of it. How do you deny that you put that on?"[30]

Maintaining Privacy

Technology experts agree that it is not difficult to maintain privacy while posting on social networks. However, before posting, these experts suggest, social networking site users should ask themselves whether the information they intend to post could possibly prove embarrassing. They should assume that their words and photos will probably be accessible to people beyond a small circle of friends, and they should understand that once they have uploaded a picture, comment, or video, just taking the offending material offline is no guarantee that it will no longer be visible. "If there is information you would not be willing to have the general public know," advises a journalist, "do not post it on Facebook."[31] The trouble is that many people find it hard to remember this guideline.

"If there is information you would not be willing to have the general public know, do not post it on Facebook."[31]

— Journalist Marie Mariem.

But even the most cautious user of Myspace, YouTube, or other social networking sites still needs to worry about privacy. The reason is that people can rarely control what other people post about them on these sites. An embarrassing photo can find its way onto the Internet even if the subject of the picture does not post it. The photographer, for a variety of reasons, might decide to upload the picture to his or her social networking pages where it is visible to almost anyone. The photographer might also choose to tag the picture, or include a caption with the subject's name. Adding the tag makes it easy for anyone looking for information on the subject to find the image. "Friends might be tagging you in photos that everyone shouldn't see" on their own Facebook pages, points out media relations specialist Heidi Sullivan, "writing about your nights on the town, or worse."[32]

An Illusion of Privacy

Although safeguarding privacy is a major problem on social networking sites, the structure of these sites can provide users with a false sense of privacy and security. Passwords, screen names, information that can be posted and removed at will—all suggest that the data that can be found on these sites is private. The sheer number of people on these sites also strongly suggests that posting is perfectly safe. With so many other posts on any given site, it may seem that one new photo, message, or video will attract virtually no attention. Indeed, one study shows that the average blog has about six readers, and that most Facebook posts are seen by hardly any more than that. "The sense online is sort of like the mob effect," says psychologist Elizabeth Englander. "You feel like you're one in a million, and so who will ever notice you?" Of course, as many people have discovered to their chagrin, it is unwise to assume that any given post will escape notice.

Quoted in Stephanie Chen, "Divorce Attorneys Catching Cheaters on Facebook," CNN, June 1, 2010. http://articles.cnn.com.

Though people who believe their privacy has been invaded in this way cannot simply take the offending images down themselves, they do have some recourse. If they are on good terms with the friend who posted the pictures, they may simply ask that the photos be removed and request further that the friend never put up similar materials again. In other cases, though, the situation is more complicated. Too often, people use their social networking sites to post pictures and comments about others for the sole purpose of causing mischief. When this happens, it can be difficult, if not impossible, to get the information removed—and the cost to the victim's reputation can be enormous.

Cyberbullies

Most experts agree that posting malicious material is especially frequent among teenagers. Much of this behavior comes under the heading of cyberbullying. "Some teens are taking great joy in capturing embarrassing images of others," writes cyberbullying expert Nancy E. Willard, "including teens being beaten up in a fight or a teen changing in a school locker room."[33] These pictures often end up on social networking sites; worse yet, the photographers usually spread the word about the images, resulting in the pictures being accessed by a steadily growing number of people and adding to the humiliation of the victims. "When they put it on the Internet," says an Indiana teenager who was victimized in just this way, "it's like they took everything and multiplied it by an astronomical number. . . . [They] are opening it up to everyone in the world."[34]

Recognizing the consequences of cyberbullying, some politicians, backed by lobbying organizations, have set out to make cyberbullying a crime. In 2009 Missouri passed a law which did exactly that, and US congresswoman Linda Sanchez of California has tried to pass a similar law on the national level. However, these bills have been controversial. Some argue that the wording is vague. Others fear that antibullying laws infringe on free speech. Even those who see cyberbullying as a serious problem do not necessarily agree that criminalizing the behavior is the best way to stop it. "We should not pass a law against cyberbullying," says author and professor John Pelfrey. "We don't want to fill our jails with teenagers who are trying to figure out how to deal with one another."[35]

Realistically, a person who is determined to post a humiliating picture of someone else on a social networking site will most likely find a way to do so. That being said, there are ways to help maximize privacy on these sites and minimize the possibility of humiliating pictures being spread across the Internet. For example, Americans can become much less tolerant of cyberbullying. Many American adults still downplay the harm caused by cyberbullies and argue that dealing with bullies of all types is just a normal part of growing up. Debbie Johnston of Florida, whose son committed suicide after several years of vicious cyberbullying, is one of many activists hoping

A 17-year-old New Yorker who teaches children about the dangers of cyberbullying, sexting, and other online hazards speaks to reporters about a new law aimed at educating children and teens about cybersafety. Cyberbullying laws have been passed or debated in several states.

to change this attitude. She likens this way of thinking to "saying rape is part of marriage"[36]—a statement with which few modern-day Americans would agree. By pointing out the cruelty of cyberbullying, Johnston and others hope to help people to be more critical of those who engage in it.

Accountability

Attempts to make social networks responsible for the content posted by users have had mixed results. Legally, companies such as Myspace and Craigslist are not liable for anything posted on their sites. According to the law, social networking sites are simply channels which provide a place for people to post; they bear no legal blame for what users choose to share. And for reasons of free speech, social networking sites have traditionally been reluctant to shut down pages because someone is offended by their content. In early 2011 in West Genesee, New York, for example, school officials tried for several months to shut down a Facebook page that mocked a number of high school students. "I've contacted Facebook myself to ask them to take the page down," reported the school superintendent. "That's been unsuccessful."[37]

But social networking sites can certainly be more responsive to people whose privacy has been violated. In the West Genesee case, Facebook officials not only refused to remove the offending page, but also refused to identify the person who posted it. School personnel responded by getting a court order to force Facebook to provide the information—a time-consuming process at best. Sites such as Facebook are understandably hesitant to provide third parties, such as school officials, with data about their posters, and they do not want to be judges of what does and does not constitute acceptable posting. Still, many experts argue that social networks can and should do more to combat invasions of privacy. The faster they respond to legitimate complaints, the less likely people will be to post reputation-damaging material.

"Any Web site allowing you to create a profile of yourself is like a public bulletin board, and one that is hanging in the seediest part of town."[39]

— Security expert Duncan Long.

Making social media companies more responsive, changing public attitudes toward cyberbullying, and bringing in the legal system may all someday be effective in safeguarding the privacy of those who use social networks. In the meantime, the best advice for keeping a semblance of privacy online is to use common sense. As a public relations specialist suggests, only partly in jest, "Avoid posing for [inappropriate] pictures in the first place."[38] And before posting anything remotely confidential to YouTube, Facebook, Myspace, or any other social networking site, security expert Duncan Long suggests keeping this in mind: "Any Web site allowing you to create a profile of yourself is like a public bulletin board, and one that is hanging in the seediest part of town. Anything posted at such a site may be examined by anyone, from the most innocent of individuals to stalkers or government agents."[39] In Long's opinion, and in the opinion of many other experts, keeping this truth in mind would reduce the number of invasions of privacy on social networking sites to nearly zero.

Chapter Three

Privacy and Corporations

In 2007 technology manufacturer Apple, Inc. released a new product called the iPhone. The iPhone was extremely versatile; in addition to making and receiving calls and texts, it had Internet capabilities, it could be used as a video camera, and it spawned a host of software applications, or apps, designed to be installed on the iPhone to make it more useful and fun. Like many other Apple products before it, the iPhone was a sensation. Within three years, Apple had sold 70 million of these devices. Apple followed up its success with the iPhone by launching another mobile device, the iPad, in 2010. A tablet computer with a touch display, the iPad proved as popular as the iPhone, if not more so. In the first year of its existence, Apple sold about 15 million iPads, accounting for more than half of all the tablet computers purchased anywhere on the globe. For Apple, the outlook seemed rosy.

In spring 2011, though, researchers Alasdair Allan and Pete Warden raised important questions about these two devices. The researchers charged that tracking software had been installed on all iPads and many iPhones as well. This software used wireless signals to monitor the location of the device at all times, even when the machine was switched off. The information was then stored in an online database. Since iPads and iPhones are designed to be portable, this meant that the movements of their owners were being tracked. However, Apple had installed the software without informing customers.

As far as Allan and Warden could tell, Apple had not used the information the devices had collected. Nonetheless, they believed that the hidden file represented a major invasion of customer privacy. In theory, at least, the information could be used in ways customers neither expected nor wanted. "By passively logging your location without your permission," the researchers explained, "Apple [has] made it possible for anyone from a jealous spouse to a private investigator to get a detailed picture of your movements."[40]

Some Apple supporters were not bothered by the research conducted by Allan and Warden. Others, however, were deeply concerned that their whereabouts were being tracked and stored. Technology expert Sam Biddle, for instance, was able to access a map of all his travels since he purchased his iPhone. He was deeply distressed at the level of detail it provided. "Everywhere I've been," he noted. "Bus trips home. Train trips to visit family. . . . My entire personal and professional life—documented by a phone I didn't know was also a tracking device." Biddle blamed Apple for not telling consumers about the tracking software. "It's just not right to have no choice in the matter," he argued. "I don't want this information bouncing around in my pocket with me."[41]

"My entire personal and professional life—documented by a phone I didn't know was also a tracking device."[41]

— Technology expert Sam Biddle.

Credit Cards and Cookies

In one sense, the Apple tracking software controversy is nothing new. Businesses have been collecting data on their customers since long before the electronic era. Prior to the invention of credit cards in the mid-twentieth century, for instance, it was common for stores to extend credit to their customers on an individual basis. To ensure that they would be paid, these stores needed to collect certain pieces of information on each of these customers. At the very least, they needed to keep a record of the customer's home address and the amount that was owed.

Still, the amount of information in customer files of the 1920s or even the 1960s is dwarfed by the amount of personal data that corporations of the twenty-first century collect about their customers. One way of collecting this information is simply to ask for it. To apply online for a credit card from the retailer Target, for instance, applicants must provide much more than names and addresses. The application also requires telephone numbers, social security numbers, birthdates, driver's license numbers, total annual incomes, monthly housing payments, the names of the banks where applicants have accounts, and the length of time they have lived at their present address.

Many corporations collect extensive data on their customers in other ways as well. When Internet users visit company websites, the website often inserts a piece of text known as a cookie onto the user's computer. The cookie can help the website recognize the computer when it next returns to the company's site, which can make Internet transactions easier and faster. However, some cookies can also track a person's online activities, such as what websites the person visits and what terms he or she types into a search engine. This information can then be reported back to the corporation that inserted the cookie to begin with. "The data harvested by the cookies is used to create a behavioral profile about a specific user,"[42] writes digital expert Chip Cooper.

"The data harvested by the cookies is used to create a behavioral profile about a specific user."[42]

— Privacy expert Chip Cooper.

Using cookies to build profiles makes sense for companies. By examining their customers' Internet activity, corporations can learn more about consumer interests and perhaps increase sales figures. Whether the profiles are in the best interest of customers, however, is another question entirely, and many privacy advocates argue that they are not. One reason is that cookies are typically installed without the computer user's knowledge or consent. Worse, though Internet users can delete most cookies if they know what to look for, some cookies are extremely difficult for even an expert to disable. Finally, some corporations sell or exchange the information they gather using cookies. Many experts argue that Internet users have a basic right to determine whether and how their personal data is used, and the installation of cookies seems to them to be a clear violation of that right.

Loyalty Cards

Loyalty cards, also known as reward cards, are another way for corporations to collect and store private information online. These cards are issued by retailers and service providers such as grocery stores and airlines. Having a card allows a customer to qualify for extra discounts, cash rebates, or free merchandise. In return, reward programs give companies easy access to customers' buying patterns. Whenever a customer uses the card to make a purchase, the customer's identifying information—hometown, age, marital status, income, and much more—is linked with details of the purchase in an online database. "These companies know where you live, what you buy . . . and how often you buy it,"[43] notes security expert Dave Methvin.

Companies use this data primarily to help them target specific customers in their advertising campaigns. If a store wants to offer discounts on baby food, for example, it can locate customers who have purchased

Businesses of all kinds collect data on their customers. The loyalty, or reward, cards commonly used in grocery stores allow customers to qualify for discounts and promotions but they also allow retailers to collect information on buying habits as well as age, income level, marital status, and more.

baby-related merchandise in the recent past. Then it can e-mail those customers with the news of its upcoming sale, while ignoring customers who never purchase these products. A merchandising cliché says that half of all advertising is wasted because the customers it is intended to reach never see it. By targeting customers based on their buying habits, companies can improve their odds of reaching the proper consumers.

"These companies know where you live, what you buy . . . and how often you buy it."[43]

— Security expert Dave Methvin.

For customers, too, loyalty cards have clear advantages. Most important, of course, is that signing up for reward programs saves customers money. In addition, many customers appreciate receiving word of other products that might interest them. Movie rental giant Netflix, for example, has developed software that analyzes customers' previous rentals and recommends other films they might like. Thus far, the software has been remarkably successful. "After six years of Netflix," writes a customer, "I almost never get a single bad recommendation, and I've been made aware of lots of films I otherwise probably wouldn't have seen."[44]

Safeguarding Data—or Not

In the United States at least, customers seem to consider providing personal data to companies a reasonable cost for the benefits they receive. One recent study suggests that nearly 60 percent of American households own at least one reward card. Privacy advocates, however, are less enthusiastic about the situation. One common concern has to do with levels of security. In many instances over the years, corporations have been unable to safeguard customer data. Some of this information is compromised by hackers—people who use a computer to gain access to supposedly private data. Sometimes, however, the problem is simple negligence. In March 2011, for example, an employee of the oil company BP lost a laptop containing unsecured personal information on about 13,000 people—and this is just one of many such incidents since the Internet age began. "One might do as well turning your private information over to the Three Stooges for safekeeping,"[45] writes Duncan Long.

Another question involves what corporations do with the data they collect. In the absence of data loss through hacking or negligence, many consumers assume that the information they share with a company stays with the company. But that is not necessarily the case. In fact, laws seldom prevent companies from selling people's private information to other corporations and to government units as well. Though some companies specifically say that they do not engage in this behavior, many others are eager to "share"—a euphemism for "sell"—their customers' private data. "We may share information about you with non-affiliated third parties whose products or services we believe may be of interest to you,"[46]

The Emotional Appeal of Loyalty Cards

By signing up for loyalty cards, people necessarily compromise some of their privacy. For many this is a fair trade; loss of privacy is outweighed by the prospect of saving money. For many shoppers, too, the emotional benefits of reward cards counteract their fears of giving up their private information. Saving money on products or earning free airline trips—especially when these perks are available only to cardholders—can help shoppers develop an image of themselves as careful, thrifty consumers. Similarly, customers often feel a sense of belonging when they join loyalty programs. This sense is reinforced by the names used for many of these programs, such as "club," "family," and "friends." Frequent visitors to properties in the Intercontinental Hotels Group, for example, join the Priority Club rather than the Priority Program, and restaurant chain Max & Erma's encourages customers to sign up for "Good Neighbor Rewards." To increase the homey touch, in fact, Max & Erma's decorates the reward program page on its website with a white picket fence. The purpose is to establish a feeling of connection between the customer and the corporation in the hope that the customer will continue to buy from the business.

Scientific American magazine informs its subscribers. Consumers often have no way of knowing what data has been sold, who has purchased it, and how the new owner intends to use it.

This is particularly worrisome because companies could easily use personal data in ways that may harm their customers. When people apply for health insurance, for instance, an insurer could buy records of the applicants' purchases at supermarkets or other retailers. Company officials could then make decisions based on the applicants' buying habits. "Those with poor diets (as demonstrated by all the soda pop and frozen pizzas they've been buying) might be singled out for physical exams," Long explains, "while those buying running shoes might get to forgo the exam when offered a policy."[47] At the moment, most observers agree that this sort of information sharing is rare, but nothing guarantees that it will remain that way.

Corporations downplay the risks to customers in collecting, storing, and sharing private information. They argue that concerns about security are exaggerated, and they insist that they do not sell personal data to companies that might misuse it. Moreover, business officials point out, web pages of corporations nearly always include privacy policies that detail how they safeguard personal information. Most of all, though, companies emphasize that a consumer who is uncomfortable sharing his or her private data with a company can simply choose not to sign up for credit cards and other offerings. As one industry representative notes, "No one forces a customer to join these customer loyalty programs."[48]

Privacy experts, however, find most of these arguments unconvincing. In addition to challenging business claims that online security is sufficient and that companies exercise restraint when selling data, privacy advocates point out that corporations often collect much more data from customers than they actually need. They also argue that online privacy policies are not especially useful to consumers. Many, they point out, are hard to find on company websites. Few customers can take the time to read privacy policies such as Symantec's, which at more than 4,000 words is longer than any chapter in this book. Even when policies are short the wording is often obscure. The privacy policy on the Farmers Insurance website, for instance, refers to "sharing nonpublic personal information" and "financial institutions with which we have joint marketing agreements."[49]

Opting Out and Opting In

In recent years privacy advocates have helped establish some safeguards for people who wish to maintain control over their private information. One of the most significant is called an opt-out provision. This feature lets customers tell corporations not to sell their personal data for any reason. Although most large retailers now allow customers to opt out, the process is not always straightforward. To exercise their opt-out provision for Farmers Insurance, for instance, customers must read the privacy policy, call a toll-free number to order a form, and wait for the form to arrive in the mail. Then they must complete the form, send it back through the post office—and wait some more: "We will implement your request within a reasonable time after we receive your form," Farmers promises.

Partly for this reason, privacy advocates would like to replace opt-out provisions with an opt-in policy instead. In this model, companies would not be allowed to share information unless customers specifically requested it. Corporations, however, are opposed to this idea. They believe that few customers would opt to have their information shared. What the future holds is anyone's guess.

Farmers Insurance, "Privacy Policy." www.farmers.com.

Google Street View

While corporations continue to ask for and sell customers' personal data, recent technological advances have helped companies find new ways to use data that some consider private. Apple's tracking software on the iPhone and iPad is an excellent example. Another well-known instance involves the Internet information company Google. In 2007 Google launched a new online feature known as Google Street View. This technology allowed computer users to see photos of the buildings and natural features along streets and highways from a street-level perspective. To do this, Google equipped vehicles with special cameras that recorded panoramic images of everything they passed. Google employees then drove the vehicles along the roads of communities across the country. Google technicians correlated the photographs with their exact locations on Google Maps. With a click of a mouse, Google Maps users had an up-close, unbroken view of the street and everything along it.

Google Street View proved quite popular at first, and Google began making good money from the project through advertising on the site. In early 2008, though, Google Street View began attracting some opposition. One of the first expressions of concern came from officials in the Minnesota city of North Oaks. A suburb of St. Paul with a population of 4,500, North Oaks has no public roads; every street in the community is privately owned by a homeowners' association to which all local property owners belong. When photos of North Oaks began appearing on Google Street View, city officials sent a sharp letter to Google complaining that the drivers had trespassed on the community's private roads. "They really didn't have any authorization to go on private property,"[50] explained the city's mayor. North Oaks requested that Google remove the photos, which Google eventually agreed to do.

"Today's satellite-image technology means that . . . complete privacy does not exist."[51]

— Attorneys for Google, Inc.

A few months later a Pennsylvania couple filed suit against Google. They charged that Google had invaded their privacy by posting a picture of their home on the Internet. The suit sought a monetary award for pain and suffering and asked the court to force Google to remove the offending picture. In this case, however, Google fought back. The company's lawyers argued that merely taking pictures and posting them online was not a violation of anyone's rights. Since modern satellites can take extreme close-up photos of homes and other buildings anywhere on the globe, Google's lawyers maintained, the expectation of privacy no longer applies as it once

The information giant Google offers online street views of locations around the globe. To make this possible, employees travel by pedal-powered vehicles (pictured) and by car with giant cameras engineered to record panoramic images. Some people feel that the street views are an invasion of privacy.

Google
Google maps
google.com/streetview
MAXXIS

did. "Today's satellite-image technology means that . . . complete privacy does not exist,"[51] Google asserted. In February 2009 a federal court agreed with Google and threw out the lawsuit.

Embarrassment and Safety

The technological sophistication of Google Street View has created other privacy-related issues as well. When Google's cameras pass any given location, they capture images of people who happen to be on the street at that moment. In a few cases, the cameras have photographed people who are doing something illegal or who are in potentially embarrassing situations. When the person in one of these pictures is readily identifiable, as has happened several times, posting the image is problematic. Privacy advocates have complained about pictures such as these, arguing that people have a right to keep their activities and movements to themselves.

Not everyone believes that posting these images constitutes an invasion of privacy. "Why do people care that they're on the Internet like this?" asks one observer. "After all, everybody else walking down the street saw them in person!"[52] Nonetheless, most people would agree that posting photos on the Internet changes the situation. It is one thing for someone to risk being seen vandalizing a mailbox or parking briefly in a handicapped spot. It is quite another to have photographic proof of those actions preserved on the Internet forever, available to anyone with an online connection. In addition, there are situations in which it could be dangerous for a person's photo to appear on the Internet. Consider the case of a woman who moves to a new city to escape an abusive husband. If he saw her picture on Google Street View, he would be better able to track her down—with potentially deadly consequences.

To fix the problem, privacy advocates urged Google to take pictures down if the people in them could be identified. Google initially resisted these efforts, but soon agreed that the advocates had a point. "It's a legitimate issue,"[53] admits Google official John Hanke. In spring 2008, in response to its critics, Google began using special software to blur faces so they are no longer recognizable in Street View pictures. The software is not perfect—it has been known to blot out the face of Colonel Sanders on KFC signs and billboards, for example—but privacy advocates applaud Google's decision to make the faces unidentifiable.

Toward Compromise

When North Oaks officials asked Google to remove pictures of their community, Google complied—but when the Pennsylvania couple took the company to court later that year, Google denied that Street View compromised the couple's privacy. When Google began posting pictures that showed real people, company leaders first defended the practice—and then agreed that it was inappropriate. These changes of heart, in a sense, are not surprising. Steering a course between the corporate need for profit and the consumer's need for privacy is tricky under any circumstance, and the advent of the Internet has made privacy issues far more complex than ever before.

At the same time, Google's uncertainty is also a hopeful sign. During the online era, corporations and advocates for privacy have rarely been in agreement. Businesses focus on how to make the most money, seeing privacy as a secondary consideration at best; privacy advocates emphasize privacy above all else. In order to determine what is best for everyone, though, it may be necessary for both sides to come together and listen to each other's concerns and insights. As Hanke puts it, the issues involved in customer privacy are neither simple nor settled. "It needs that debate," he says. "We see that and try to let it play out."[54] In the end, having that debate—and in as open a way as possible—will be essential if the tension between corporate interests and privacy rights is to be resolved.

Chapter Four

Privacy and Government

In 1949 British writer George Orwell published his most famous book, a novel called *Nineteen Eighty-Four*. The book describes a future society in which government has taken almost total control of its people. In the novel, government officials tell their citizens what to do, what to think, and what to feel. Language itself is under government control, stripped of ordinary meaning in slogans such as "WAR IS PEACE/FREEDOM IS SLAVERY/IGNORANCE IS STRENGTH."[55] A group called the Thought Police roams the country, looking for those whose ideas do not match those permitted by the government. Indeed, citizens exist to serve the state, individual identity has been nearly stamped out, and the government is all that matters.

For many readers, the most disquieting aspect of Orwell's novel is the government's ability to spy on every one of its citizens. The government uses a variety of methods to reach this goal. Government agents routinely intercept letters written from one citizen to another, for example, scanning the messages for indications of independent thought or other subversive activity. Other agents masquerade as ordinary citizens, arresting people whose loyalty to the state seems lacking. Government leaders encourage citizens to observe one another closely for signs of rebellion. Even children are told to turn their parents in if the situation demanded. "It was almost normal for people over thirty to be frightened of their own children," Orwell writes. "And with good reason."[56]

The most effective surveillance, however, is accomplished by means of telescreens—one-way windows with audio capability that have been placed in almost every home, office, and outdoor gathering place. The telescreens permit government leaders to watch and hear citizens' activities in all of these locations. The telescreens are far from a secret; indeed, the state constantly reminds its citizens that they are being observed. The supposed leader of the government is a man known as Big Brother, and his face appears on posters throughout the country, accompanied by the

The chilling image of a government that spies on its citizens and encourages them to spy on each other lies at the heart of Nineteen Eighty-Four *by George Orwell (pictured at his typewriter in a German wax museum exhibit). The rise of the Internet has heightened concerns about government intrusion in people's private lives.*

statement "BIG BROTHER IS WATCHING YOU."[57] Together with the reading of private letters and the threat of being arrested on the word of an undercover agent or a child, the telescreens have succeeded in robbing every citizen of every vestige of a private life.

Nineteen Eighty-Four is fiction, of course, and Orwell did not intend it to be an accurate prediction of life a generation or two removed from his own time. Nor was it, as it turned out. The year 1984 came and went without much evidence that countries such as the United States were becoming just like the world of Orwell's novel. That is still the case today. Only the most virulently antigovernment Americans would argue that the United States of the early twenty-first century is the equivalent of Orwell's fantasy world. No presidential administration has ordered the installation of telescreens in private homes or workplaces. No posters remind people that they are forever under surveillance. Elections are still free; dissenting opinions are still permitted; and parents do not worry that their children will denounce them to the police.

"BIG BROTHER IS WATCHING YOU."[57]

— Author George Orwell.

Nonetheless, Orwell's description of the world of *Nineteen Eighty-Four* has some parallels to modern life, particularly where the right to privacy is concerned. The reason is the rapid growth of technology since Orwell wrote his masterpiece. The rise of the computer and the enormous popularity of the Internet have made it more and more possible for governments to monitor their citizens' private lives, should they wish to do so. True, a computer is not a telescreen, a global positioning system is not designed to be a government spy, and the Internet is not fundamentally a way to intercept mail. But living in a digital age certainly makes it easier for a government, intentionally or not, to invade the privacy of its citizens. And the potential results of a government attack on privacy are enough to give many Americans pause.

A History of Mistrust

Even before Orwell wrote *Nineteen Eighty-Four*, Americans had a long history of viewing governments of all types—and especially the federal government—with some suspicion. Indeed, distrust of government has been a theme in American life for as long as the country has been in existence. One of the rallying cries of the American Revolution, after all, was "No taxation without representation,"[58] an expression of protest against the British government and its treatment of the colonists. After achieving independence, moreover, Americans first formed a union under the Articles of Confederation, a document which purposely gave the national government very little authority. Though the Constitution gave more power to the federal government, even the Constitution included checks and balances and a Bill of Rights to ensure that the national government could not become too strong. And ever since the Constitution went into effect more than 200 years ago, Americans have gone back and forth be-

The Downingtown Scandal

Government agencies are often victimized by hackers—computer experts who access information without authorization. One well-known case from 2008 involves a 15-year-old student who attended Downington High School West in suburban Philadelphia. The student managed to download to a flash drive the names and social security numbers of over 40,000 people who lived in the Downington school district. The breach of security was detected soon afterward, and the student responsible for the hacking was quickly identified—as were several friends with whom he had shared the information. Fortunately, it appears that the student never actually used the social security numbers. "We recovered the flash drive that [the hacker] had used," explained a district official, "and we believe the information was contained to those few students." Although this hacker did not benefit financially by accessing private data, his actions exposed a serious flaw in the school's security systems.

Quoted in Suzette Parmley, "Student Hacks District Files," *Philadelphia Inquirer*, May 17, 2008. http://articles.philly.com.

tween relying heavily on government and deeply mistrusting everything it stands for.

Much of the mistrust has been related to government's ability to collect information about its citizens, especially its ability to collect this information without citizen consent. Certainly governments of all kinds collect quite a variety of information from the people they represent. Privacy advocates, moreover, would point out that much of this data would qualify as private. Motor vehicle offices gather birth dates and home addresses of people who register their cars with the state or apply for driver's licenses. Taxing authorities store taxpayers' social security numbers to ensure that tax payments are credited to the correct person. School districts fingerprint prospective employees and check online registries to make sure they are not hiring convicted child molesters. The files of federal, state, and local government agencies include a wealth of personal information about nearly every adult American.

Most Americans would agree that collecting this data is not a problem in itself. Without the ability to gather and store information about residents, after all, governments would be unable to function. Even the smallest municipality, school system, or sewer district requires access to personal data to do its job. There is not much point in having a police force that is forbidden to keep records on people it has arrested, for example. A school district has every right to collect the home addresses and birth dates of its students, if only to establish that students are district residents and are placed at the appropriate grade level. And it is hard to imagine a public library remaining in existence for long if people are allowed to borrow books and other materials without identifying themselves.

Indeed, Americans often support the collection of private data by governments, as long as it is collected for certain purposes. Chief among these goals is the fighting of crime, especially terrorism. The USA PATRIOT Act, passed overwhelmingly by Congress soon after the terrorist attacks of September 11, 2001, increased the federal government's power to monitor people's activities without their knowledge. The stated goal was to improve efforts designed to catch and track terrorism suspects. The law included provisions expanding the government's ability to listen to private phone conversations, simplifying the procedure for the government to examine a suspect's belongings, and perhaps most important, letting federal agents obtain records of a suspect's Internet use. "The FBI can ask Internet service providers to turn over a log of the web sites a person visits and the addresses of e-mail coming to and from the person's computer,"[59] explains a public policy website.

Yet Americans can also be stubbornly reluctant to trust governments with their personal data. In 2009, for example, US representative Michele Bachmann announced that she would refuse to fill out most of her US census form in 2010. Many of the questions on the form, she explained, were "very intricate, very personal,"[60] and she believed that the answers were not the business of the federal government. In 2011 US senator Patrick Leahy introduced a bill to limit the federal government's

A California public library warns patrons that under the USA PATRIOT Act federal law enforcement agencies may be able to obtain records of books and other materials borrowed. Bills have been introduced to limit the government's ability to obtain this information.

ability to access a library patron's borrowing records without the patron's knowledge. Bachmann, a staunch conservative, and Leahy, a strong liberal, rarely see eye to eye on political questions. But as these actions indicate, each representative has serious concerns about allowing government easy access to information.

Government and the Internet

The rise of the Internet has only increased concerns about protecting privacy from government prying and abuse. One reason is the ease of accessing data that is stored online and in electronic form. Like businesses, governments once kept all their records in card files and ledger books. Even 50 or 60 years ago it was a major undertaking for the typical government office to locate, sort, and make use of its stored information. Now, however, digital files and online databases make it possible for governments to pull up stored information about any given resident with a few mouse clicks. Nor do government officials need to be in the same physical space as the data in order to access it. On the contrary, the information is available from any office run by that agency—and in some cases, from an Internet-connected computer in a coffee shop or public library.

Another reason involves the type of data that can be obtained and stored in today's world. In 1949, when *Nineteen Eighty-Four* was published, people understood that devices such as the telescreen could only exist in fiction. The technology of the period was not advanced enough to build an actual model. Today, though, much of what used to qualify as science fiction has become reality. There may not be any telescreens, but satellites orbiting the earth can snap detailed photos of towns and cities—and beam them back to the governments that want the pictures. Likewise, police forces and other government bodies are increasingly able to set up security cameras in public places. "Every street in New York has a surveillance camera,"[61] says Emily Nussbaum, using some exaggeration to make her point. These cameras can be used to monitor the comings and goings of

> **"Every street in New York has a surveillance camera."[61]**
>
> — Author Emily Nussbaum.

A Stolen Laptop

Just as businesses have occasionally lost sensitive information that has been stored electronically, so too has government. One day in 2006 a data analyst with the Department of Veterans Affairs brought a laptop home from work. A remarkable amount of private information on veterans was stored on the machine and its external hard drive; the data included names, birth dates, and social security numbers for over 26 million former members of the military. The databases on the laptop also included information on more than 2 million active duty service members.

Given the sensitive data on the laptop, permitting an employee to carry the computer to and from work was risky. Certainly department officials came to regret this decision. While the laptop was in the analyst's home, it was stolen. Though the computer was recovered intact eight weeks after the theft, and forensic teams found the databases had not been accessed, this largest information security breach in US history was a fiasco for federal officials. Senator Susan Collins of Maine called the incident "simply appalling," and the government eventually paid $20 million to settle a lawsuit by veterans who had been exposed to possible identity theft.

Quoted in Duncan Long, *Protect Your Privacy*. Guilford, CT: Lyons, 2007, p. 48.

ordinary people in a way that would have been difficult, if not impossible, in Orwell's time.

And the Internet makes other types of government surveillance feasible. By surreptitiously placing special software on someone's computer, for example, government officials can monitor that person's keystrokes and learn his or her passwords, browsing habits, and instant messaging contacts. Similarly, governments can intercept and read e-mails as they are sent between unsuspecting parties. Government officials can even use software that automatically scans these e-mails for certain words and phrases. Governments of today might be most inclined to search for words such as *bomb*, which might indicate potential terrorist acts; but the software can be rigged to seek out any words government officials choose. E-mails that contain enough of the key words can be flagged and set aside for further study. Given these advances in technology, the world of the early twenty-first century is not perhaps as far from Orwell's grim vision as we might wish.

Laws and Loopholes

In an effort to stave off the potential excesses of government surveillance, the United States has a number of ways to limit government's ability to gather information. One of the most powerful of these involves warrants. A warrant is a document issued by a judge; it represents official permission for a police agency to search the contents of a person's home, record a person's private conversations, or otherwise infringe on that person's privacy rights. To get a warrant in a particular case, a police force must convince the judge that it has good reason to believe the person in question is a potential suspect in a crime. If the judge cannot be convinced, no warrant is issued.

In addition to warrants, several pieces of legislation have helped to constrain the power of government where privacy rights are concerned. Perhaps the most important of these laws is the Privacy Act of 1974. Among other features, this landmark piece of legislation limits the amount of private information government agencies may share with one another. For example, the law affects the ability of US Census Bureau officials to share information it collects on specific Americans with immigration authorities, police forces, or indeed any other arm of government. As a government website puts it, "It is against the law for the Census Bureau to give personally identifiable information about an individual to any other individual or agency until 72 years after it is collected."[62] Other forms of sharing data among agencies are similarly disallowed.

But the law has some important loopholes. Perhaps most notably, the Privacy Act does not forbid government agencies from sharing data with private companies. As a result, governments at all levels frequently sell the personal data of their citizens to businesses. The Oklahoma state government, for example, brings in about $13 million each year by selling Oklahomans' private information, much of it stored in online databases listing motor vehicle owners and holders of driver's licenses. According to an Oklahoma newspaper account, "Birth dates and other personal information flow freely on a daily basis [from the state] to insurance companies, employment screening services . . . attorneys, individuals and more."[63]

> **"Birth dates and other personal information flow freely on a daily basis [from Oklahoma government] to insurance companies, employment screening services . . . attorneys, individuals and more."[63]**
>
> — Journalists John Estes and Paul Monies.

Nor do government officials necessarily take the time to ensure that the buyers of the information are trustworthy. "We don't go out and run a big background check on somebody that walks in and tries to get an MVR [motor vehicle record],"[64] admits an official at the Oklahoma Department of Public Safety, which maintains databases of driver's licenses and car registrations. Moreover, once the information has been sold to a private business, the data can be resold to other buyers; the government no longer controls it. In a bizarre twist, the data gleaned from the records of one government agency can even end up at a second government office. While Oklahoma's Department of Public Safety is barred from selling its online records directly to a second government office, nothing prevents it from taking the private data it collects and selling it to a business, which in turn sells it to the second office. The process is certainly contrary to the spirit of the Privacy Act, but it is perfectly legal—and far from rare.

Especially in a time when governments are suffering from severe budget shortfalls, the sale of data to private companies may be somewhat justified. The $10 or so Oklahoma makes from the sale of each record, after all, is money that does not come out of taxpayers' pockets. Despite the extra income, though, privacy advocates are troubled by the notion that governments can share information at will. In their opinion, citizens should be able to control the flow of their data. If a company offers to buy a database containing a person's driving record, privacy advocates argue, that person should be able to veto the sale if he or she chooses to keep the information private. Moreover, they add,

POLICE DEPARTMENT
CITY OF NEW YORK
SECURITY
CAMERA
7-1637
NYPD
PELCO
165
31st St

Surveillance cameras have been installed in major cities around the world to help law enforcement track terror suspects and solve crimes. Tens of thousands of security cameras can be found at intersections, such as this one, in New York City. Some consider these cameras to be intrusive.

people own their private information; governments do not. The bulk of the money earned from the sale of private data to corporations should go to the people whose data is being sold, not to the government.

Police Power and Monopoly

In some ways, this debate is not very different from the debate over privacy and businesses. Indeed, people who worry that businesses collect too much information from customers typically have the same concerns about governments. That being said, the situations are not identical. No one is required to sign up for a pharmacy loyalty card or to visit a particular retailer's website. Customers can choose which companies to do business with, and they are able to use corporations' privacy policies to help them decide. If they fear that one supermarket will not adequately protect their personal data, they are welcome to patronize a different one. In contrast, Oklahoma residents who own cars or trucks must submit their personal data to the state's Department of Public Safety. There is no competing motor vehicle department on the next block. Even if they suspect that the state will not keep their private information secure, they have no other options.

In addition, governments have powers that private businesses do not: the ability to arrest people, fine them, and put them in jail. It is that power that makes the constant surveillance in Orwell's *Nineteen Eighty-Four* so alarming. A business that spies on its customers, perhaps by tracking the websites they visit, might in theory use this data to embarrass consumers. A government that engages in identical behavior can use the information in the same way—but the government can also make arrests if it does not like what it sees. Governments in several countries, most notably China, have a long history of imprisoning people after subjecting them to surveillance. In these nations, unfortunately, the surveillance can be for almost any reason.

To be sure, governments in the United States very rarely exercise these powers against people who are not already under suspicion of committing crimes. Still, such abuse of power is hardly beyond the realm of imagination. This is not to say that the United States is in any danger of becoming like Orwell's imaginary country of *Nineteen Eighty-Four* anytime soon. What it does mean is that government, more than business, more than social networking sites, more than any other institution in American life, has a remarkable ability to destroy privacy—and can do so with devastating results. As a consequence, it is reasonable for Americans to work especially hard to keep all their governments fair and consistent, and to be sure no government misuses its power by abusing the privacy of any of its citizens.

Chapter Five

Hackers

In 2006 the Japanese entertainment giant Sony launched the PlayStation Network, an online system that allowed users to play video games against other members of the network. The network grew rapidly; by March 2011 the system had about 77 million members. Therefore, Sony's announcement in April 2011 that the security of the PlayStation Network had been compromised was a major news story. Although information stored on the network was supposed to be off-limits to outsiders, someone had found a way to access this data online.

While Sony did not share all the details of its investigation right away, the company admitted that the data the perpetrator had viewed probably included customer credit card numbers and possibly included card billing addresses and birth dates. A computer security expert describes the situation as "one of the worst breaches [of security] we've seen in years."[65] Sony closed the network and suggested that customers cancel the credit cards they had used to open their accounts. As of late May 2011, it was not yet clear who had compromised the company's security system—or how.

What happened to Sony is a classic example of computer hacking, or obtaining unauthorized access to a protected website. Though the sheer number of compromised records in the Sony case sets it apart from most other instances of hacking, similar breaches of privacy and security are actually quite common. Many of these breaches, moreover, are carried out for the express purpose of stealing data from unsuspecting individuals and companies. The result is that computer hacking has become a very big business. While it is difficult to estimate the monetary cost of the stolen data, in the United States alone, hackers walk away with information worth billions of dollars every year.

Computer hacking has become big business. Hackers breached the Sony Corporation's PlayStation Network in 2011, compromising customer records that may have included names, addresses, birthdates, and credit card numbers belonging to 77 million members.

Cyberthieves

People who use the Internet to steal credit card numbers, social security identifiers, and other personal information are often called cyberthieves. Cyberthieves can use the data they steal in a variety of ways. Many sell the information they collect. Plenty of criminals are willing to pay, sometimes quite well, for personal data that has been obtained by hackers. A single credit card number, for instance, might sell for $10 or $20, while a social security number might fetch $50 or more. Others use the credit card numbers themselves, ordering merchandise online or by phone and arranging to have items sent to an address that is not the victim's. They continue with this buying spree until reaching the card's spending limit, or until the card's owner recognizes that the number has been stolen.

Other cyberthieves are less interested in credit cards and more interested in social security numbers, driver's license numbers, and birth dates. These people are known as identity thieves. Their goal is to amass as much data as possible about an unsuspecting person. Then they use that person's identity to obtain credit cards and other documents in the victim's name. The process is not difficult; a thief does not require much information to pretend to be somebody else. "In order to apply for a credit card," explains Internet safety expert Latanya Sweeney, "the key things I need are your name, your date of birth, your address, and your SSN [social security number]."[66] A hacker who has successfully penetrated a corporate database, a government website, or an individual's computer files can get all four of these pieces of data easily enough.

The next step is to apply for a credit card, usually online, using the stolen information to support the application. If the victim has a decent credit history, the odds are good that the card will be issued. The cyberthief can then have the card and all associated bills mailed to a different address. The victim has no immediate way of knowing what has happened, and the thief can run up bills on the credit card at his or her leisure. It often takes at least three months before the victim discovers the fraud, and it can take much longer. To make matters worse, if the bills are not paid—and of course the thief has no incentive to pay them—the victim's credit score will suffer.

Cyberthieves can also access bank accounts and other financial data. The results in these cases are even more economically devastating for victims than are cases of credit card fraud. In some cases, identity thieves have made repeated withdrawals from victims' bank accounts totaling hundreds of thousands of dollars before the theft was discovered. "The average bank robber may be lucky to get away with $5,000, and face a 10-year prison sentence if he's caught," explains identity theft expert Robert J. Hammond, contrasting the ease of identity theft with the risks of more traditional crimes. "Using a computer, smart identity thieves can withdraw more than 10 times that amount on a daily basis, without leaving a trace. No hidden cameras. No clues. No fingerprints."[67] In short, the Internet has been an enormous windfall to identity thieves.

Identity Theft

Identity theft existed long before the Internet. Anyone whose wallet or purse was stolen, or whose home was burglarized, was a potential victim. But the Internet has provided criminals with new ways to access information and has made it possible for thieves to steal personal data on a larger scale. The Internet has also made it easier for a thief to use stolen information to his or her advantage. Prior to the digital age, for example, draining a victim's bank account usually required a thief to withdraw funds in person. It was entirely possible that the teller knew the victim and would recognize that the thief was an imposter. Today, when banking is often done electronically, that risk is much reduced. Similarly, the rise of Internet retailing has made it increasingly possible for thieves to use credit cards without ever handing them over to a merchant for scrutiny.

"The average bank robber may be lucky to get away with $5,000, and face a 10-year prison sentence if he's caught. Using a computer, smart identity thieves can withdraw more than 10 times that amount on a daily basis, without leaving a trace."[67]

— Identity theft expert Robert J. Hammond.

The result is that in the twenty-first century, identity theft has become a major problem. According to one study, about 10 percent of Americans have been victimized by identity thieves, and information theft affects approximately 10 million Americans in any given year. Not all of these thefts involve computer hacking, but many of the most damaging are committed via the Internet. The stakes are high. In a typical year, thieves

Online banking is easy and convenient, but theft of personal data—either through hacking of poorly secured sites or through online scams—can be a major problem for consumers. In a typical year, more than 2 million Americans discover that their bank accounts have been compromised.

Manage your money online

New User

Register my existing account

Apply for a new account

Why bank online?

Try our demo

Register for Employee Share Schemes

Existing User

Username

Password

Your mother's first name?

Sign in

Remember my username*

*Do not select if this computer is used by anyone else. More information about storing usernames

Read more

Problems signing in?

Forgotten sign in details / access suspended?

HELP US TO HELP YOU
STAY SECURE ONLINE

If you are not a UK resident, or are trying to access this site from outside the UK, please read this **important message**

Halifax plc, Registered in England No.2367076. Registered Office: Trinity Road, Halifax, West Yorkshire, HX1 2RG

Online service ...

AP Server

obtain the social security numbers of 3 to 4 million different Americans, and more than 2 million Americans discover that their bank accounts have been compromised. Incidences of identity theft are growing, too. "The odds have never been higher for becoming a fraud victim,"[68] says a researcher, noting that reports of identity theft rose nearly 40 percent between 2007 and 2009.

"The odds have never been higher for becoming a fraud victim."[68]

— Security expert James Van Dyke.

Nor is it a simple matter for consumers to repair the damage done by identity theft. According to one study, victims can expect to spend more than 300 hours calling credit bureaus, contacting banks, and carrying out other activities in an attempt to straighten out the mess. As Hammond points out, this process is made more difficult because victims often do not receive much sympathy. "The prevailing attitude of most creditors advised of a case of identity fraud is downright suspicion,"[69] Hammond writes. Many victims are never fully able to erase the consequences of the theft from their credit reports; some have difficulty qualifying for loans in the future. Moreover, out-of-pocket expenses associated with repairing the harm can easily top $1,000—and this is in addition to any permanent financial losses from unauthorized access to bank accounts and credit cards.

Obtaining Information

Many cyberthieves who troll for personal information use the strategy of the people who obtained unauthorized access in the Sony case: They hack into the databases stored in the computer systems of a large business or a government agency. As the Sony example demonstrates, this method can reap enormous rewards for a hacker who manages to bypass the system's security features. Obtaining 77 million credit card numbers, after all, is no small feat—and the potential payoff of such an attack is huge. Indeed, some of the best-publicized cases of information theft have involved hackers who have made their way into corporate and government files to steal personal information.

One recent example involves Rogelio Hackett, a perhaps appropriately named hacker from Georgia. Beginning in 2002 and continuing for

Hackers as Heroes

Today, hackers are seen as a serious threat to privacy and order. But this was not always true. In 1983, soon after hacking reached the public consciousness, hackers were thought of almost as folk heroes. The movie *War Games*, released that year, told the fictional story of a young man who hacks into a Department of Defense supercomputer and almost starts a nuclear war. The main character, played by actor Matthew Broderick, was portrayed in a sympathetic light despite his illegal activities and the potential consequences of his actions. That same year a group of teenagers and young adults known as the Milwaukee 414s (the number referred to Milwaukee's area code) briefly became famous for accessing dozens of supposedly secure networks. Though these networks included systems used at high-level government laboratories, many Americans were more amused than enraged by the group's activities. One of the 414s was even featured on a *Newsweek* magazine cover, with an accompanying caption that read "Trespassing in the Information Age: Pranks or Sabotage?" For plenty of Americans at the time, the answer to *Newsweek*'s question was clear: Hacking was simply a prank.

Newsweek, September 5, 1983.

seven years, Hackett routinely raided online databases to steal credit card numbers and other information from customers. When he was arrested in 2009, authorities found that he had over 675,000 credit card numbers on file, most of them stolen in just this way. These thefts were quite lucrative for Hackett. Though the exact amount he stole is disputed, credit card companies believe he made tens of thousands of fraudulent charges on these accounts for a total of at least $36 million. In April 2011 Hackett admitted his guilt in court. He faced the possibility of heavy fines and up to 10 years in prison.

Hacking into corporate files figured in an even larger theft shortly before Hackett's arrest. In May 2008 a New Jersey corporation called

Heartland Payment Systems was victimized by an attack on its computer databases. Heartland processed payments for other corporations and merchants, so it had hundreds of thousands of credit card numbers and other financial data stored in its electronic files. To make matters worse, Heartland did not realize until early 2009 that its security had been breached. "This is a very sophisticated attack,"[70] Heartland's president admitted when the news broke. The company eventually acknowledged that the hackers had accessed approximately 130 million pieces of data. As of spring 2011, this remains the largest theft of private information in history.

Phishing and Passwords

Battling the onslaught of computer hackers is an army of corporate, government, and academic experts in Internet security. The bigger the network, the more sophisticated its security systems are likely to be. And when security breaches occur, wealthy corporations such as Heartland and Sony can devote considerable resources to determining who is responsible. Indeed, Hackett is not the only hacker to be arrested for mining corporate files in search of personal data. Albert Gonzalez, the hacker who masterminded the Heartland attack, was sentenced to a 20-year prison term in early 2010.

Because of the risks and difficulties of accessing information through corporate or government databases, many hackers target individuals instead. While this strategy is less lucrative, it may ultimately be more effective. Hackers use a variety of methods to uncover private information from ordinary citizens. One of these is known as *phishing*. In this scheme, hackers send out e-mails that look as if they come from banks, social networking sites, or other legitimate businesses. The e-mails typically assert that there is a problem with the recipient's account; they often include alarming statements such as "If you don't respond within 48 hours, your account will be closed."[71] In order to fix the problem, the recipient of the e-mail is told to click on a link that will bring up a particular website. Once on the website, the consumer is instructed to provide an account password, an updated credit card number, social security number, or some other personal data.

Just like the e-mails, the websites may look authentic. Indeed, the links provided may seem to be for a legitimate corporation or government agency. But they are not. Clicking the link actually brings the consumer to a different website, one that has been created by cyberthieves. Once unsuspecting customers enter their personal information on the website, cyberthieves can read the information from the web page and use it to make purchases on credit cards, drain bank accounts, and establish new identities. In a more sophisticated version of this scam, visiting the website causes the victim's computer to download a keylogging program and install it on the machine without the consumer's knowledge. This program allows cyberthieves to secretly record every keystroke the

FBI officials discuss the arrest of dozens of people involved in phishing attacks on thousands of people. Fraudulent e-mails that appear to come from banks, social networking sites, or other legitimate businesses seeking account numbers and other information are known as phishing scams.

computer's owner makes, providing them with passwords, account numbers, and other private information.

Some hackers take a different approach. They try to figure out the passwords that people use for online banking and similar activities on the Internet. Security experts say this is a surprisingly simple task. Computer users often select passwords that are all too obvious: They use their names, series of repeated digits such as 7777, or common words like *love* and *princess*. One recent study suggests that the sequence 123456 accounts for over 1 percent of all passwords used in the United States. These passwords are easy to guess, giving cyberthieves access to all kinds of private information. "That means never using passwords such as 'welcome' or 'password,'" advises an article in the magazine *Consumer Reports*. "Instead mix up letters and numbers to make for tougher encryption."[72]

"Never use passwords such as 'welcome' or 'password.' Instead mix up letters and numbers to make for tougher encryption."[72]

— *Consumer Reports.*

Common Sense and Government Mandates

To some degree, common sense and caution can help ordinary consumers keep their private information out of the hands of cyberthieves. Using strong passwords, with random strings of digits and letters, can be very effective. So can installing a password on a home wireless network. "Encrypting your network . . . is an important step toward identity theft prevention,"[73] advises Maryland attorney general Douglas Gansler. Consumers should take the advice of security experts and never send passwords, social security numbers, or bank account information via e-mail. Moreover, they should check all incoming e-mails from corporations and governments thoroughly to make sure that the e-mails are not actually phishing scams. Internet users should be especially suspicious of links in these e-mails that send consumers to websites where they can enter information, since the link may not lead to a legitimate site even if it appears to do so. When in doubt, suggests *Consumer Reports*, "don't click on such links; type the correct Web address into the browser."[74]

Causing Chaos

Not all hacking is aimed at obtaining the private information of individual computer users. In fact, many hackers are more interested in causing damage to computer systems than in any personal gain. For these hackers, the whole purpose is to see how much chaos they can cause. Some of these hackers create viruses—self-replicating programs that can damage data drives and destroy information—and send them out to computer networks. The "downadup" virus, released by a hacker in 2009, has since spread to at least 3.5 million computers worldwide, causing system errors, loss of data, and other problems. And the Stuxnet virus, which began spreading in 2010, caused particular anxiety among security experts when it began sabotaging Iran's defense systems. According to officials at Kaspersky Lab, an Internet security firm, "Stuxnet is a working—and fearsome—prototype of a cyber-weapon, that will lead to the creation of a new arms race in the world."

Kaspersky Lab, "Kaspersky Lab Provides Its Insights on Stuxnet Worm," September 24, 2010. www.kaspersky.co.uk.

Unfortunately, even the most secure of home computers cannot fully protect an Internet user from losing their private information to hackers. For that matter, even people who never use the Internet are at risk of having their personal data compromised. That is because so many corporations and government entities store private information online. In modern America, almost any activity—getting a driver's license, registering to vote, using a credit card, and on and on—will result in personal data appearing in an electronic file, there for the taking by a clever hacker. And while individual computer users can take steps to secure data on their own computers and networks, they are at the mercy of whatever security measures these larger organizations choose to adopt.

Partly as a result, governments around the world are beginning to mandate certain basic levels of security for corporate databases. In the

United States, for instance, medical providers and health insurers are required to demonstrate that they have taken steps to safeguard patient information. The requirements include limiting access to databases, writing and following privacy policies, and encrypting e-mails and other communications. Several European countries have gone further. In 2010 the United Kingdom fined two large companies more than $1.5 million each for failing to protect customers' private data. These incidents demonstrated that the UK was adopting a tougher stance toward companies that did not do enough to prevent identity theft. "Organisations will have to take security more seriously," says a British analyst. "It is clear [the government] is prepared to punish in a meaningful way."[75]

Good News and Bad

The good news is that security is becoming ever stronger. Just as locking a car door can discourage a casual car thief, increased security and more caution can keep unsophisticated and less determined cyberthieves from accessing personal information. Some experts believe that web users today are significantly safer from this kind of hacker than they were in the early 2000s. But if measures of this sort can scare away casual hackers, they are not so effective when it comes to deterring highly knowledgeable and creative hackers. Even the most advanced security system may yield to a cyberthief who is willing to spend hundreds or thousands of hours developing a plan to defeat it. With each improvement in security, hackers simply learn new tricks. "The attackers have the upper hand in this cat-and-mouse game,"[76] concludes a report from an Internet security corporation.

While that conclusion is not pleasant to hear, it should also come as no surprise. Cyberthieves, after all, are criminals, and the reality is that crime of all kinds is difficult to eradicate. People who think they can enrich themselves through crime will always be tempted to operate outside the law, and cyberthieves are no exception. The past decades have seen enormous advances in home security systems, for example—and yet burglaries continue to be a problem. Laws restricting guns and lengthening minimum prison sentences have not eliminated armed robbery, and improved methods of detecting financial crimes have not prevented securities fraud and embezzlement.

Viewed in this light, the stealing of private data over the Internet will probably never completely go away. People do what they can to reduce the chances of being burglarized or robbed at gunpoint, while recognizing that there is always a risk. In the same way, consumers should take reasonable measures to safeguard their private information—but they must also be aware that complete peace of mind in this regard is probably impossible.

Source Notes

Introduction: The Complexities of Privacy

1. Quoted in Carolyn Thompson, "Open WiFi Can Lead to Trouble," *Poughkeepsie (NY) Journal*, April 25, 2011, p. 5A.
2. Richard Wortley and Stephen Smallbone, "Child Pornography on the Internet," Center for Problem-Oriented Policing, 2006. www.popcenter.org.
3. Illinois Attorney General, "Madigan: Lake County Man Arrested on Child Pornography Charges," January 8, 2011. www.illinoisattorneygeneral.gov.

Chapter One: Privacy and the Internet

4. Quoted in Angelica Bonus, "Pennsylvania School District Settles Laptop Privacy Lawsuit," CNN, October 12, 2010. http://articles.cnn.com.
5. Quoted in Cory Doctorow, "School Used Student Laptop Webcams to Spy on Them at School and Home," *Boing Boing,* February 7, 2010. www.boingboing.net.
6. Quoted in *Philadelphia Daily News*, "Lower Merion School District Sued for Cyber Spying on Students," February 18, 2010.
7. Quoted in CBS News, "Did School Spy on Kid at Home via Webcam?," February 19, 2010. www.cbsnews.com.
8. Quoted in Michael D. Simpson, "Big Brother Goes High Tech," National Education Association, August 2010. www.nea.org.
9. Quoted in Susan Phillips, "Specter Calls for Law to Prevent Webcam Snooping," WHYY News and Information, March 29, 2010. http://whyy.org.
10. Quoted in John R. Vile, *A Companion to the United States Constitution and Its Amendments*. Santa Barbara, CA: Praeger, 2010, p. 162.
11. US National Archives and Records Administration, "United States Constitution." www.archives.gov.
12. Electronic Privacy Information Center, "Public Opinion on Privacy." http://epic.org.
13. Justin_Bailey, "Agreed," post to Straight Dope Message Board, February 18, 2010. http://boards.straightdope.com.

14. Duncan Long, *Protect Your Privacy*. Guilford, CT: Lyons, 2007, p. xxi.
15. Quoted in Jonathan Shaw, "The Erosion of Privacy in the Internet Era," *Harvard Magazine*, September/October 2009. http://harvardmagazine.com.
16. *Consumer Reports*, "Online Exposure," June 2011, p. 31.
17. Quoted in Bobbie Johnson, "Privacy No Longer a Social Norm, Says Facebook Founder," *Guardian* (Manchester, UK), January 11, 2010. www.guardian.co.uk.
18. Quoted in Polly Sprenger, "Sun on Privacy: 'Get Over It,'" *Wired*, January 26, 1999. www.wired.com.
19. Quoted in Zoe Kleinman, "How Online Life Distorts Privacy Rights for All," BBC News, January 8, 2010. http://news.bbc.co.uk.
20. Quoted in Shaw, "The Erosion of Privacy in the Internet Era."
21. Long, *Protect Your Privacy*, p. 164.

Chapter Two: Social Networking

22. Quoted in *Daily Local News* (Chester County, PA), "Phillies Visit White House to Celebrate World Series Win," May 15, 2009.
23. Quoted in espn.com, "Facebook Post Gets Worker Fired," March 9, 2009. http://sports.espn.go.com.
24. Quoted in espn.com, Facebook Post Gets Worker Fired."
25. Steve Kovach, "How to Go Completely Invisible on Facebook," *Business Insider*, January 19, 2011. www.businessinsider.com.
26. Quoted in Eric Frazier, "Facebook Post Costs Waitress Her Job," *Charlotte (NC) Observer*, May 17, 2010. www.charlotteobserver.com.
27. Marie Mariem, "The Effects of Too Much Facebook Exposure," Helium.com, February 18, 2010. www.helium.com.
28. Quoted in Erin Moriarty, "Did the Internet Kill Privacy?," *CBS Sunday Morning*, February 6, 2011. www.cbsnews.com.
29. Nitrozac and Snaggy, *The Joy of Tech*, December 5, 2007. www.geekculture.com.
30. Quoted in Stephanie Chen, "Divorce Attorneys Catching Cheaters on Facebook," CNN.com, June 1, 2010. http://articles.cnn.com.
31. Mariem, "The Effects of Too Much Facebook Exposure."
32. Heidi Sullivan, "Top 10 Tips on How to Avoid a Professional Embarrassment on Facebook," Cisionblog, November 12, 2008. http://blog.us.cision.com.

33. Nancy E. Willard, *Cyber-Safe Kids, Cyber-Savvy Teens*. San Francisco: John Wiley and Sons, 2007, p. 99.
34. Quoted in Janet Kornblum, "Cyberbullying Grows Bigger and Meaner with Photos, Video," *USA Today*, July 14, 2008. www.usa today.com.
35. Quoted in David Pogue, "Q&A: Rumors, Cyberbullying and Anonymity," *New York Times*, July 22, 2010. http://pogue.blogs.nytimes.com.
36. Quoted in Kornblum, "Cyberbullying Grows Bigger and Meaner with Photos, Video."
37. Quoted in 9WSYR.com, "Update: Offensive Facebook Page About West Genesee Students in Flux." www.9wsyr.com.
38. Quoted in Sullivan, "Top 10 Tips on How to Avoid a Professional Embarrassment on Facebook."
39. Long, *Protect Your Privacy*, p. 180.

Chapter Three: Privacy and Corporations

40. Quoted in John D. Sutter, "Report: iPhones Secretly Track Their Users' Locations," CNN.com, April 21, 2011. www.cnn.com.
41. Quoted in Sutter, "Report: iPhones Secretly Track Their Users' Locations."
42. Chip Cooper, "Flash Cookies Trigger Privacy Suits Against Online Marketers," Digicontracts. www.digicontracts.com.
43. Quoted in Long, *Protect Your Privacy*, p. 45.
44. Mark Hughes, "Do People Find Netflix's Recommendations Algorithm Useful in Practice?," Quora, April 12, 2011. www.quora.com.
45. Long, *Protect Your Privacy*, p. 47.
46. "Privacy Policy," *Scientific American*, January 26, 2010. www.scienti ficamerican.com.
47. Long, *Protect Your Privacy*, p. 51.
48. Adriana Noton, "Retail Marketing Programs for Winning Customer Loyalty," Business and Marketing Strategies, December 12, 2010. www.writeplace.info.
49. Farmers Insurance, "Privacy Policy." www.farmers.com.
50. Quoted in Steven Musil, "Minnesota Town Tells Google Maps to Get Lost," CNET News, June 1, 2008. http://news.cnet.com.
51. Quoted in Steven Musil, "Google Wins Street View Privacy Suit," CNET News, February 18, 2009. http://news.cnet.com.

52. Paulej, comment, Stephen Shankland, "Google Begins Blurring Faces in Street View," CNET News, May 13, 2008. http://news.cnet.com.
53. Quoted in Shankland, "Google Begins Blurring Faces in Street View."
54. Quoted in Shankland, "Google Begins Blurring Faces in Street View."

Chapter Four: Privacy and Government

55. George Orwell, *Nineteen Eighty-Four*. New York: Harcourt Brace, 1949; Fairfield, IA: 1st World Library, 2004, p. 23.
56. Orwell, *Nineteen Eighty-Four*, p. 34.
57. Orwell, *Nineteen Eighty-Four*, p. 7.
58. Quoted in Steven Laurence Danver, ed., *Revolts, Protests, Demonstrations, and Rebellions in America*, Santa Barbara, CA: ABC-CLIO, 2010, p. 145.
59. Constitutional Rights Foundation, "The Patriot Act." www.crf-usa.org.
60. Quoted in Stephen Dinan, "Minn. Lawmaker Vows Not to Complete Census," *Washington Times*, June 17, 2009. www.washingtontimes.com.
61. Quoted in Shaw, "The Erosion of Privacy in the Internet Era."
62. Hillsborough County, Florida, "Frequently Asked Questions," 2010 Census Information.www.hillsboroughcounty.org.
63. Quoted in John Estes and Paul Monies, "Oklahoma Brings in Millions by Selling Personal Data," *Oklahoman* (Oklahoma City), April 4, 2010. http://newsok.com.
64. Quoted in Estes and Monies, "Oklahoma Brings in Millions by Selling Personal Data."

Chapter Five: Hackers

65. Quoted in *Poughkeepsie (NY) Journal*, "Sony: Credit Card Data at Risk in PlayStation Hack," April 27, 2011.
66. Quoted in Shaw, "The Erosion of Privacy in the Internet Era."
67. Robert J. Hammond, *Identity Theft: How to Protect Your Most Valuable Asset*. Franklin Lakes, NJ: Career, 2003, pp. 32–33.
68. Quoted in Jennifer Waters, "The Rise of Identity Theft: One Man's Nightmare," *MarketWatch*, February 10, 2010. www.marketwatch.com.
69. Hammond, *Identity Theft*, p. 19.

70. Quoted in Byron Acohido, "Hackers Breach Heartland Payment Credit Card System," *USA Today*, January 23, 2009. www.usatoday.com.
71. Microsoft Safety and Security Center, "How to Recognize Phishing Email Messages or Links." www.microsoft.com.
72. *Consumer Reports*, "Your Security: 25 Things Cops and Crooks Say You're Doing Wrong," June 2011, p. 20.
73. Quoted in Maryland Attorney General, "Attorney General Gansler Advises Consumers to Protect Personal Information on Wireless Networks." www.oag.state.md.us.
74. *Consumer Reports*, "Your Security," p. 20.
75. Quoted in Bill Goodwin, "Tougher Compliance Rules Will Force Data Security Improvements," *Computer Weekly*, January 28, 2011. www.computerweekly.com.
76. Websense Security Labs, *Security Trends Report*, 2005, p. 13.

Facts About Online Privacy

- According to the June 2011 *Consumer Reports*, 15 percent of Facebook account holders post their current locations or their plans for travel.
- ABC News reports that a stolen credit card number can be sold on the black market for $2 or $3. Platinum cards and other high-limit cards can fetch up to $20.
- As reported in Ashlee Vance's article "Simple Passwords Remain Popular" in the January 21, 2010, *New York Times*, one out of every five passwords used on the Internet is simple and easy to guess, such as "qwerty" or "abc123."
- Hackers typically take less than four minutes to enter a computer system, reports Jonathan Shaw in the September 2009 issue of *Harvard Magazine.*
- Banks, insurance companies, and credit card issuers, notes the organization Privacy Rights, are required by law to allow consumers to opt out of having their data shared with other organizations.
- According to the Electronic Privacy Information Center (EPIC), Google stores users' search terms, together with their IP addresses, for 18 months.
- Privacy Rights Clearinghouse notes that in a 2010 case called *U.S. v. Warshak*, a court ruled that the government must obtain a search warrant before reading individuals' e-mails.
- A Zogby International poll discovered that half of Americans say they are very concerned about the possibility of identity theft.
- EPIC notes that collecting personal information from a child under age 13 is against the law unless the child's parent consents.
- According to Parsons and Oja's *New Perspectives on Computer Concepts, 2010*, Internet Explorer, like several other Internet browsers, can be set to a variety of privacy and security preferences.

- In a 2010 survey, EPIC reports, Facebook scored in the bottom 5 percent of US companies for customer service, in part because of issues of keeping members' data private.

- Jonathan Shaw in the September 2009 issue of *Harvard Magazine* notes that some experts believe that Internet crime costs Americans $1 trillion a year.

- In her article "Identity Theft Nightmare," written for marketwatch.org, Jennifer Waters reports that incidents of identity theft rose by 37 percent between 2007 and 2009.

- According to EPIC, a health care worker who sells confidential patient information can be fined up to $250,000 or jailed for up to 10 years.

- The article "Illinois Rakes in Millions Selling Personal Data," originally published in the *Bloomington (IL) Daily Pantagraph*, reports that Illinois makes over $60 million a year selling its citizens' personal data to insurance companies and other businesses.

Related Organizations

Association for Competitive Technology
1401 K St. NW, Suite 502
Washington, DC 20005
phone: (202) 331-2130
website: http://actonline.org

This international organization is an association of information technology businesses. It lobbies on behalf of its members and encourages innovation in business and technology. It is often reluctant to support laws which strengthen privacy rights because of fears that such laws will disrupt commerce and limit consumer choices.

Bureau of Consumer Protection
600 Pennsylvania Ave. NW
Washington, DC 20580
phone: (202) 326-2222
website: www.ftc.gov/bcp

A division of the Federal Trade Commission, the Bureau of Consumer Protection collects complaints about consumer fraud and identity theft and makes them available to law enforcement agencies across the country. Under the consumer information tab, the website has many publications regarding online privacy and security.

Electronic Frontier Foundation
454 Shotwell St.
San Francisco, CA 94110-1914
phone: (415) 436-9333
fax: (415) 436-9993
e-mail: information@eff.org
website: www.eff.org

One of the first organizations established to support privacy rights in the online world. It provides information on laws relating to Internet privacy and works to ensure that governments and industries respect privacy rights.

Electronic Privacy Information Center (EPIC)

1718 Connecticut Ave. NW
Washington, DC 20009
phone: (202) 483-1140
fax: (202) 483-1248
website: http://epic.org

This organization focuses on safeguarding privacy in the digital age. It emphasizes traditional civil liberties. Its website includes articles and links to other useful sites.

Electronic Retailing Association

2000 N. 14th St., Suite 300
Arlington, VA 22201
phone: (800) 987-6462
fax: (703) 841-8290
e-mail: info@retailing.org
website: www.retailing.org

This group advocates for online retailers. The organization lobbies political leaders for laws that are favorable to forming connections between customers and businesses online.

International Association of Privacy Professionals

Pease International Tradeport
75 Rochester Ave., Suite 4
Portsmouth, NH 03801
phone: (603) 427-9200 or (800) 266-6501
fax: (603) 427-9249
website: www.privacyassociation.org

This is an organization made up of people who work on privacy policies and similar matters for law firms, banks, and other corporations. The group's website offers details about changes in privacy laws as well as links to related articles.

Internet Alliance

1615 L St. NW, Suite 1100
Washington, DC 20036-5624

phone: (202) 861-2407
e-mail: tammy@internetalliance.org
website: www.internetalliance.org

A nationwide group that advocates for the Internet industry. It lobbies for legislation that makes Internet commerce easier. It is intended primarily for businesses and government policy makers.

Netchoice

1401 K St. NW, Suite 502
Washington, DC 20005
phone: (202) 331-2130
fax: (202) 331-2139
e-mail: info@netchoice.org
website: www.netchoice.org

A trade organization made up largely of online retailers and service companies, Netchoice attempts to make business on the Internet easier to conduct. In particular, it lobbies Congress for the elimination of laws its members see as burdensome.

Ponemon Institute

2308 US 31 North
Traverse City, MI 49686
phone: (231) 938-9900
fax: (231) 938-6215
e-mail: susan@ponemon.org
website: www.ponemon.org

The Ponemon Institute conducts independent research on privacy, data protection, and information security policy.

Privacy Rights Clearinghouse

3100 5th Ave., Suite B
San Diego, CA 92103
phone: (619) 298-3396
fax: (619) 298-5681
website: www.privacyrights.org

This organization is mainly concerned with the privacy rights of consumers. It offers information on issues such as identity theft, protecting the privacy of medical records, and ensuring that banks and other financial institutions do not divulge personal information to third parties without the consent of consumers.

The Public Voice

e-mail: coney@epic.org
website: http://thepublicvoice.org

An arm of the Electronic Privacy Information Center (EPIC), this organization focuses on the future of the Internet and the gathering of information worldwide. The website includes a number of articles and alerts about online privacy.

For Further Research

Books

Federal Trade Commission, *Net Cetera: Chatting with Kids About Being Online.* Washington, DC: Federal Trade Commission, 2009.

Grant Greenberg, *Facebook and Privacy: What You Need to Know to Keep Your Privacy Safe*. Kindle Edition. Amazon Digital Services, 2010.

Duncan Long, *Protect Your Privacy.* Guilford, CT: Lyons, 2007.

Daniel J. Solove, *Nothing to Hide: The False Tradeoff Between Privacy and Security*. New Haven, CT: Yale University Press, 2011.

———, *Understanding Privacy*. Cambridge, MA: Harvard University Press, 2008.

Raymond Wacks, *Privacy: A Very Short Introduction.* New York: Oxford University Press, 2010.

Nancy E. Willard, *Cyber-Safe Kids, Cyber-Savvy Teens*. San Francisco: John Wiley and Sons, 2007.

Periodicals

Consumer Reports, "Your Security," June 2011.

Jared Keller, "The Facebook Privacy Wars Heat Up," *Atlantic*, May 6, 2010.

Steve Lohr, "How Privacy Vanishes Online, a Bit at a Time," *New York Times*, March 17, 2010.

Jonathan Shaw, "The Erosion of Privacy in the Internet Era," *Harvard Magazine*, September/October 2009. http://harvardmagazine.com/2009/09/privacy-erosion-in-Internet-era?page=all.

Internet Sources and DVD

Facebook Etiquette and Privacy for Dummies!, DVD, Wiley, 2009.

Marie Mariem, "The Effects of Too Much Facebook Exposure," Helium.com, February 18, 2010. www.helium.com/items/1745997.

Websites

Electronic Privacy Information Center (http://epic.org). Includes articles and news items about issues relating to electronic privacy from a civil liberties perspective.

Facebook Privacy Policy page (www.facebook.com/policy.php). Describes Facebook's privacy policies, which have influenced similar policies throughout the online business and social networking worlds.

Privacy Rights Clearinghouse (www.privacyrights.org). Articles, information, and links relating to the privacy of consumers, both on- and offline.

Index

Note: Boldface page numbers indicate illustrations.

Picture Credits

Cover: Thinkstock/Photodisc
Maury Aaseng: 19
AP Images: 23, 25, 39, 45, 49, 65, 69
© Iason Athanasiadis/Corbis: 8
© Viviane Moos/Corbis: 58
Yuriko Nakao/Reuters/Landov: 62
© Kurt Rogers/San Francisco Chronicle/Corbis: 53
© Joseph Solm/Visions of America/Corbis: 15
Roger L. Wollenberg/UPI/Landov: 33

About the Author

Stephen Currie is the author of several dozen books for young adults and other readers. He has also written magazine articles, educational materials, and other works, and he has taught levels ranging from kindergarten to college. He lives with his family in New York State.